second

Believing
and Living

For WJEC specification B, Unit 1

Gavin Craigen
and Joy White

 HODDER
EDUCATION
AN HACHETTE UK COMPANY

The Publishers would like to thank the following for permission to reproduce copyright material:

Photo credits
p.2 NASA; **p.3** *soap, phosphorous, nail, sugar, water* Life file/Emma Lee, *lime* Geoscience Features, *magnesium* Science Photo Library/Russ Lappa, *potassium* Science Photo Library/Astrid & Hanns-Frieder Michler, *sulphur* Science Photo Library/Charles D Winters; **p.4** Photolibrary Group Ltd/Brand X; **p.5** Fotolia/Wimbledon; **p.10** NASA; **p.11** Corbis/Stuart Westmorland; **p.15** Science Photo Library/John Sanford; **p.16** Science Photo Library/Claude Nuridsany & Marie Perennou; **p.20** Studio Photogram, Inc./BLOOMimage/Getty Images; **p.21** Reuters/Guillermo Granja; **p.27** Ann & Bury Peerless; **p.28** Jewish National Fund; **p.29** Alamy/Yadid Levy; **p.30** Alamy/Yaacov Shein; **p.34** True Love Waits; **p.38** *l* Alamy/BlueMoon Stock, *cl* Photofusion/Jacky Chapman, *cr* Corbis/Fancy/Veer, *r* Alamy/Tetra Images; **p.39** True Love Waits; **p.42** *l* Rex Features/Albert Michael, *r* PA Photos/Daniel Miller/AP; **p.50** *l* PA Photos/George Nikitin, *r* Corbis/Rick Friedman; **p.58** John Rifkin; **p.61** *t* Photolibrary Group Ltd./Photodisc, *b* iStockphoto.com/©Lucwa; **p.65** Circa/John Smith; **p.66** Circa/John Smith; **p.67** *t* Peter Sanders, *b* Circa/Barrie Searle; **p.69** *Humanist symbol* British Humanist Association; **p.72** *t* PA Photos/Rajesh Kumar Singh/AP, *c* Circa/John Smith; **p.73** *cl* Corbis/Dave Bartruff, *cr* Circa/Ged Murray, *b* Corbis/Bob Rowan/Progressive Image; **p.74** *tl* Corbis/Peter Turnley, *tr* Circa/Ged Murray, *c* Circa/William Holtby, *bl* Peter Sanders, *br* Ann & Bury Peerless; **p.75** *tl* Christine Osborne Pictures, *tr* Tzedek UK, *c* Format/Jacky Chapman, *b* ISKON Educational Services/Food for All; **p.79** *t* Photolibrary Group Ltd/Photodisc, *b* iStockphoto.com/©Lucwa; **p.82** AKG London; **p.84** Peter Sanders; **p.90** Corbis/Peter Turnley; **p.92** *tl* Corbis/Robert Van Den Berge/Sygma, *tr* Getty Images/Sam Panthaky/AFP, *cl* ISKON Educational Services, *cr* Rex Features/Mark Campbell, *bl* Photofusion/Pam Isherwood, *br* PA Photos/Tony Harris; **p.94** Salvation Army; **p.95** Gavin Craigen; **p.96** Catholic Association for Racial Justice; **p.97** *l* Illustrated London News, *r* Corbis/Earl & Nazima Kowall; **p.98** *t* Food for Life; *b* Food for All; **p.99** *l* Circa/John Smith, *r* Reuters/Vasily Fedosenko; **p.100** *c & b* Reproduced with permission of Islamic Relief Worldwide; **p.101** *l* Corbis/Richard T. Nowitz, *r* Corbis/Nik Wheeler; **p.103** *tl, tr & b* Tzedek UK; **p.104** *bl & br* Karuna Trust; **p.105** Sikhcess; **p.106** *ct* Christian Aid, *cr* Tearfund, *cl* CAFOD; **p.110** Show Racism The Red Card; **p.111** *tl* Circa/John Smith, *tr* Peter Sanders, *cr* Rex Features/Jussi Nukari; **p.112** *t* Christine Osborne Pictures, *bl* Alamy/Michael Freeman, *br* Christine Osborne; **p.113** Every Life Counts/The Greise Youth Theatre; **p.114** Reuters/Reinhard Krause; **p.117** Alamy/EmmePi Images; **p.118** Reproduced with permission of Islamic Relief Worldwide; **p.119** Steve Derby/Tzedek UK; **p.120** Karuna Trust; **p.121** Sikhcess.

Text acknowledgements
The Publishers would like to acknowledge use of the following extracts:

P.16 'Who Made a Mess?', taken from *The Day I Fell Down the Toilet* by Steve Turner, published by Lion Publishing; p.27 article adapted from an article by Let the Animals Live (Israel), 25 September 2008, www.letliveorg.il/english; p.50 article adapted from 'Male Priests Marry in Anglican Church's First Gay "Wedding"', The Telegraph, July 2008; p.58 Prayer for Agunot, International Coalition of Agunah Rights; p.71 extract from 'Guardian Angel' from *A Hand on my Shoulder* by N. Cook and V. Frampton, New Cherwell Press, Oxford.

Every effort has been made to trace all copyright holders, but if any have inadvertently been overlooked, the Publishers will be pleased to make the necessary arrangements at the first opportunity.

Although every effort has been made to ensure that website addresses are correct at time of going to press, Hodder Education cannot be held responsible for the content of any website mentioned in this book. It is sometimes possible to find a relocated web page by typing in the address of the home page for a website in the URL window of your browser.

Hachette Livre UK's policy is to use papers that are natural, renewable and recyclable products and made from wood grown in sustainable forests. The logging and manufacturing processes are expected to conform to the environmental regulations of the country of origin.

Orders: please contact Bookpoint Ltd, 130 Milton Park, Abingdon, Oxon OX14 4SB. Telephone: (44) 01235 827720. Fax: (44) 01235 400454. Lines are open 9.00–5.00, Monday to Saturday, with a 24-hour message answering service. Visit our website at www.hoddereducation.co.uk

© Gavin Craigen and Joy White 2009
First published in 2001 by
Hodder Education,
Part of Hachette UK
338 Euston Road
London NW1 3BH

This second edition first published 2009

Impression number   5
Year   2013

Illustrations by Peter Bull/Peter Bull Art Studio
Cover photo: Daly & Newton/The Image Bank/Getty Images
Typeset by Fakenham Prepress Solutions, Fakenham, Norfolk NR21 8NN
Printed in Dubai
A catalogue record for this title is available from the British Library.

ISBN: 978 0340 975 572

Contents

1 Our world

The Big Picture

What makes us human?
How did the universe begin?
How should animals be treated?
Why are we here?
How and why can we use our talents?
How should we use natural resources?
How and why should we care for the world?

Questions to ask

Religious teachings to explore

- Creation
  – Creation stories and their meaning
- Using talents
- Place of humankind in the world
  – Purpose of humankind in the world
  – Stewardship issues in terms of the current exploitation of the planet
- Animal rights
- Care for the world and the environment
  – Example of a religious individual or community using talents for God, neighbour and care of the planet

Check it out

The definitions in these boxes in this chapter are basic outlines only; always add an appropriate example in your explanation, and remember the context is religious believers.

What makes us human?

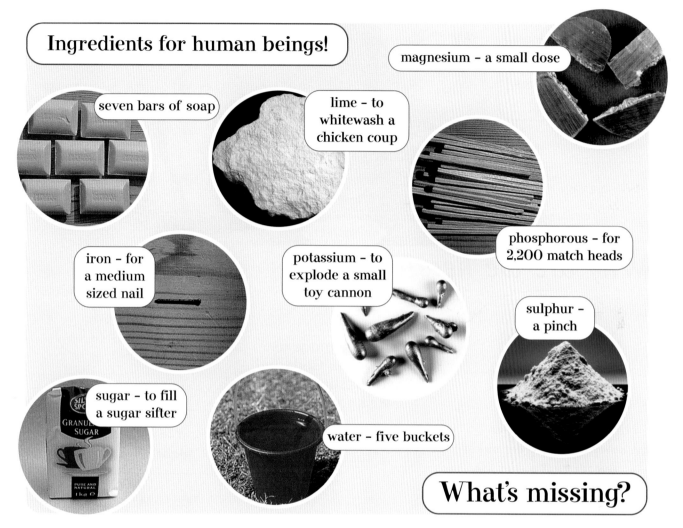

Ingredients for human beings!

magnesium – a small dose

seven bars of soap

lime – to whitewash a chicken coup

phosphorous – for 2,200 match heads

iron – for a medium sized nail

potassium – to explode a small toy cannon

sulphur – a pinch

sugar – to fill a sugar sifter

water – five buckets

What's missing?

When we start asking questions about ourselves, we find there are many different aspects that make us the people we are.

We have **bodies** that grow and help us live and move;

We have **minds** to think and decide;

We have **personalities** that make us different from other people;

We have **emotions** through which we react;

We also have **experiences** and **influences** that affect the kind of people we are and the decisions we make.

Task

- What are your major influences?
- Rank in order these influences in your life.

friends · family · teachers · school · community · fashion · laws · books · religion · television · magazines · newspapers · music

Why are we here?

To try and make the world a better place.

People do not live nowadays; they get about ten per cent out of life.

❝You have made us to know you, God, and we die restless until we know you.❞

(St Augustine)

Someday I want to be rich.

To do all the things I want to do and go all the places I want to go.

Check it out

Always add examples

Humanity

Compassion for others e.g. by serving others voluntarily

Caring about other human beings through prayer and action

People give many reasons as to why we exist, but some, whether they are religious or not, believe it is important for humanity to care about each other and for the planet.

All religions teach that human beings are unique and different from all other animals.

INTELLIGENCE	the ability to think and reflect; to apply knowledge and learning; to reason
MORALITY	a sense of right and wrong; values
LANGUAGE	the ability to write/read languages; use of learned languages

Christians would add that another important difference is revelation. By this they mean that humanity is:

Created in God's image; capable of religious behaviour and beliefs; having a conscience; in possession of a 'soul'.

 Explain what religious believers mean by 'humanity'. [2]

Look at the two answers below. Which do you think is better, and why?

Answer A	Answer B
Human beings; being kind hearted.	The way in which human beings care about other people because that is how God meant them to live.

Answer A was awarded 1 mark and Answer B, 2 marks.

Can you explain why?

Can you think of other possible answers?

Exam Tip

When answering a question about the meaning of a key concept, remember two things:

- **explain**, do not just state – so you need to include reasons or causes; you are explaining the **why** behind something.

- the answer is about **religious believers** – so you need to give an example that reinforces your explanation.

Check it out

Always add examples

Soul

What is the soul?
Many Christians believe the soul is:

That part of human nature that is not just physical

The part of humans that will live on after the body has died

A reflection of 'the image of God' in human beings

The part of humans that allows people to relate to God; and to worship

The spiritual aspect of human nature that affects the 'real' you

5

Religious teachings about the place and purpose of humankind in the world

Throughout many religious and sacred books we read how humanity has a number of purposes and responsibilities in life:

For Christians:
- to serve God and live for him. *(This includes telling others about and sharing one's faith.)*
- to obey God. *(Following the way of life His commandments show and which Jesus taught.)*
- to enjoy the world and its fruits/resources. *(They are a gift from God.)*
- to look after the world for God (stewardship). *(This includes sensible use of resources and trying to conserve nature.)*
- to look after and live in harmony with others. *(This is also a way of serving God, by serving others in a selfless unconditional way.)*
- to have sexual relationships and children. *(This is seen as natural and a God-given ability and calling.)*

For Jews:
- to obey God. *(This includes observing the Commandments.)*
- to enjoy the world and its fruits/resources. *(This includes seeing God in them; and being responsible in use.)*
- to look after the earth for God (stewardship). *(This is being in charge on behalf of God.)*
- to preserve trees. *(Not destroying them wildly, especially in times of war or dispute.)*
- to live in harmony and care for others. *(Loving your neighbour as you love yourself).*
- to have sexual relationships and children. *(This is a God-given blessing.)*

For Hindus:
- to perfect one's wisdom, and heart and mind. *(So as to free the atman from the physical body.)*
- to live so as to fulfil one's dharma. *(This is an important and vital aspect of everyone's life.)*
- to seek the truth. *(That which lies beyond the material, the impure, the illusory.)*
- to practise harmlessness (ahimsa). *(Not harming any living thing.)*
- to amass good karma. *(Through duty, devotion or other deeds or path to liberation.)*
- to gain moksha. *(Freedom from samsara, the cycle of life.)*
- to have sexual relationships and children. *(These are a natural part of life; being a parent is one of the stages of life (ashramas) for most people.)*

For Muslims:
- to live for Allah alone. *(There is no God but Allah.)*
- to respect other human beings and animals *(for there is one creator of all).*
- to act as khalifahs or guardians of the planet *(for Allah gave this responsibility to humans).*
- to have sexual relationships and children. *(This is a natural part of life and a gift from Allah.)*

For Sikhs:

- to achieve union with God (mukti). *(This is liberation from the cycle of birth and death.)*
- to meditate on God's name, focusing heart and mind on God. *(This is becoming god-centred gurmukh.)*
- to serve others selflessly. (Sewa.)
- to earn an honest living. *(Known as Kirat Karna; it is an obligation and a necessity.)*
- to have sexual relationships and children. *(These are a normal part of life, and are an implanted characteristic by God into all human beings.)*

For Buddhists:

- to grow and experience freedom and happiness. *(This includes following the teachings of the Buddha, the Eightfold Path.)*
- to deepen one's understanding. *(This is about wisdom and intention.)*
- to follow the five precepts. *(The moral guidelines to life.)*
- to train the mind to lead to nirvana. *(This is about effort, mindfulness, concentration.)*
- to escape from the wheel of life. *(Through positive choices and decisions.)*
- to have sexual relationships and children. *(These are natural parts of life, and caring for parents and children is seen as the highest blessing.)*

Using our talents

Everyone has talents – things that they are good at doing, certain skills or abilities that they have, and some people like to use or demonstrate those talents.

If God gave you the talent, you should go for it. But don't think it's going to be easy. It's hard!
Aaliyah (American singer)

I wrote the Brotherhood song for no money out of my deep feelings about humanity, and because I was flattered that whatever talents I had, had been recognised.
Tom Glazer (American singer)

A winner is someone who recognises his God-given talents, works his tail off to develop them into skills, and uses these skills to accomplish his goals.
Larry Bird (American sports coach)

All our talents increase in the using, and every faculty, both good and bad, strengthens by exercise.
Anne Brontë (British author of 'The Tenant of Wildfell Hall')

Most religious believers feel talents or skills they have should be used and developed. They often believe that such talents are given by God. Failure to develop them or use them for the benefit of others would be seen as not only wasteful, but as an insult to God.

I believe God gave me my musical ability. I love playing the piano, and wherever I play, it is both worship and a witness.

The Buddha taught it is important to show compassion (karuna), so I use my talents to look after the elderly.

It is my duty to serve Allah and use my talent as a lawyer. What I do I try to do well, not only because I live for Allah alone, but also because it benefits others, and shows them what being a Muslim is.

I have natural talents, and so it is my dharma to use them and live as a good citizen, helping others and seeking the truth; they are good, positive things.

It's my mitvah or duty to use the talents God has given me to carry out good deeds.

I use my God given talents for service or sewa, not just in the Gurdwara, but to all those in need.

Exam Tip

Always use key concepts and specialist language in your answers to questions.

Q *Explain the teachings about looking after the world in* **one** *religious tradition.* [6]

Look at the two answers below, and using the Levels of Response Grids on page 123, decide what marks you would give to Answer A and Answer B, and why.

Answer A	Answer B
Muslims believe that **Allah** made the world and everything that is in it. Humans are seen as the most important, and are understood to be **khalifahs**, or trustees, as it says in **Surah** 6:165 'He has made you His ruling agents in the earth'. It is therefore **humanity's responsibility** to maintain the pattern and balance (or **fitrah**) in the world. To do this requires humans to actively use their skills to look after the **environment** and not allow it to be spoiled. Islam regards this as very important, and humans will be questioned about their 'caretaking' for Allah on the **Day of Judgement**.	Christians would look after the world and all the animals because they are told to in their special book. They think that **God** gave them this job to do, so that's why they do it.

Task

- Take Answer B and rewrite the answer using at least five of the key concept or specialist language terms.

How did the universe begin?

Throughout human history, people have asked this question.

To many religious people there is little doubt that God is the cause or creator of the universe.

As humans have discovered more and more about the universe, so scientists began to construct theories about its beginnings. To some people it seemed that such ideas replaced the beliefs in God as the originator of all things.

There are many different views as to how the universe began. Within Christianity, Hinduism, Islam, Judaism, Sikhism and Buddhism, we find stories of creation which are often interpreted in different ways.

Creation in Judaism 🕎 and Christianity ✝

the 1st day

the 6th day

the 2nd day

the 7th day -holy

the 5th day

the 3rd day

the 4th day

Jews and Christians share the same story of Creation, found in Genesis 1 and 2. In this story it makes clear the belief that God created everything that is in the heavens and the earth:

Check it out

Always add examples

Creation

A unique design, planned by a maker

God's making of the world for a purpose

- Light and dark
- Sun, moon and stars
- Day and night
- All kinds of living creatures
- Time and seasons
- Human beings
- Land, sea and sky.

> ❝And God looked at all that he had created, and behold, it was good.❞
>
> (Genesis 1:31)

All these were created in 'six days', and on the seventh day God rested.

There are different responses to this story within Christianity and Judaism.

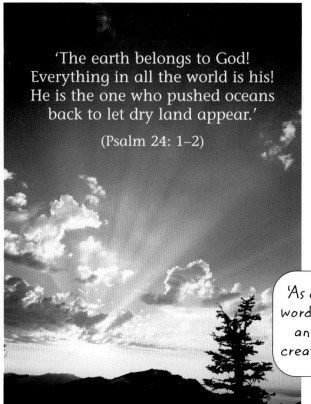

'The earth belongs to God!
Everything in all the world is his!
He is the one who pushed oceans
back to let dry land appear.'

(Psalm 24: 1–2)

'I am a practising Christian but do not believe every detail of the creation happened like it says in Genesis. The importance of the story is not how God created the earth, but that he did!'

Helen, age 16

'As a Christian I believe every word in the Bible is true. Yes it's an amazing story about the creation — but God is amazing!'

Mark, age 18

Literalist views e.g. Mark	**Non-literalist views** e.g. Helen	
The main points of the story actually happened the way they are described – literally: ● God's spirit moved across the waters. ● There were six days of 24 hours in which God created. ● Adam was formed out of the dust of the earth. ● Eve was formed out of Adam's rib. *Believers of this view see a conflict between science and religion, and are convinced of the truth of the Bible in a literal and fundamental sense.*	The main point of the story is not to detail *how* God created, but to state that he did. So the story is not a literal account, but does contain important truths – such as: ● God did create the world. ● That he used the natural processes he created. ● That there were clear 'periods' of creation, though not 24 hours as such. *People who accept this view, see no real conflict between scientific theories and religion, and can see how both weave together to give a full picture of life and the earth.*	The story is entirely poetic and/or mythical. It is not true, and contains no literal truth, but is describing what the writers of the time believed to be true. Scientific knowledge and discovery have shown the ideas of creation to be unacceptable. *People who think this believe that scientific explanations, based on evidence and research, are irrefutable, and that religious ideas are a different (and less trustworthy) kind of statement.*

Whatever position a person takes, it would seem true to say that, in general, Christians and Jews would agree that the Genesis story illustrates some important key beliefs:

- *God created everything for a purpose.*
- *The beginning of the world and of life was not accidental.*
- *Human beings are different from other creatures, in being in the 'image of God', and sharing some responsibility for the world.*
- *That the world created was basically good.*

The stories of creation . . . are not intended to teach scientific truths, as we would understand them today. They are actually intended to teach religious truths. For example, they teach us that the universe was created by God, that it didn't just come into existence on its own, and that the universe as a whole is good.

(Professor Nancy Murphy, speaking on *The Question Is . . . ?* video)

Q *Explain the beliefs from* **one** *religious tradition about the world and the purpose of human beings.* [6]

Task

- On the right is an answer that gets 2 marks. What would you add to give it Level 4 and 6 marks? (see the Levels of Response Grids on page 123)

Name of religious tradition: **Judaism**

Beliefs about the world and the purpose of human beings: Jews believe God created the earth and that humans were given the job of being stewards for God. They also believe it is each person's responsibility to do mitzvot, or good deeds, in the world. Jews also have rules about the environment – food laws and things like that.

Creation in Islam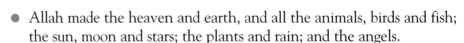

- Allah made the heaven and earth, and all the animals, birds and fish; the sun, moon and stars; the plants and rain; and the angels.
- The angels were sent to bring seven handfuls of earth – each of a different colour.
- From these the first man, Adam, was made; and from his side, Eve – the first woman.
- They lived in Paradise – a beautiful garden; where they could eat anything, except the fruit of one tree.
- On disobeying Allah, after being tempted by Iblis they were placed outside the garden as a punishment.

Muslims believe that human beings were given the role of *khalifah* or guardian/steward to look after the earth and treat it with respect.

This responsibility is a binding duty on the whole community of Muslims (*ummah*). Muslims come from many countries and speak a wide range of languages, but they were all created by Allah and are expected to follow the *Shariah* (the Islamic law based on the Qur'an and Sunnah).

Muslims are expected to actively keep the delicate natural balance of the environment – the key to survival. This is considered such an important role that on the Day of Judgement, all Muslims will be called into account for how they have looked after Allah's creation.

> He had made you His ruling agents in the earth, and has given some of you higher rank than others, so that He might test you in the gifts He has given you. Your Lord is quick to punish, but also He is forgiving and merciful.
>
> (Surah 6:165)

Creation in Sikhism

- God is the creator of all things.
- He existed before the world.
- Before the world was created there was only deep darkness.
- God brought the universe into being.
- God is present in all created things, including humans (though he is much more than those things).

Sikhs believe that the world was brought into being by God deliberately. Because God is love, he created the world as a gift of love, and it is something that humans can enjoy.

They do not see that their beliefs are against scientific beliefs, as they also believe that the world was created to grow and develop, or evolve. Guru Nanak talked about a universe that was 'ever becoming'.

Creation in Hinduism ॐ

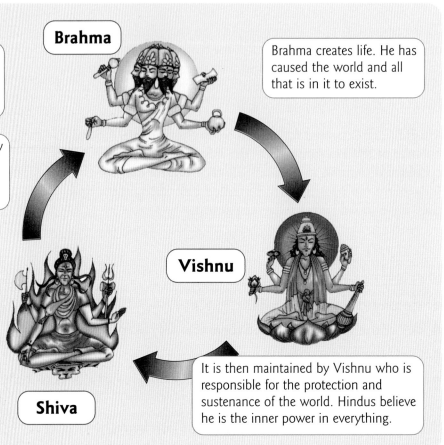

Brahma

However, Lord Shiva is also the recreator and so when all is turned to dust once more the cycle of life continues.

And the next universe is ready to be born. So follows the endless cycle of creation and destruction.

Brahma creates life. He has caused the world and all that is in it to exist.

Vishnu

However, there comes a time when almost all the universe is evil and so the time for the universe to die. This is when Shiva appears in fire and wind, and everything dies before him. The universe crumbles to dust.

Shiva

It is then maintained by Vishnu who is responsible for the protection and sustenance of the world. Hindus believe he is the inner power in everything.

When God prepared
the sacrifice with
Purusha as their
offering,
Its oils was spring, the
holy gift was autumn,
Summer was the wood.
They balmed as victim
on the grass,
Purusha,
Born in earliest time ...

- Creation is *anandi* (that which has no beginning) and that it is eternal.

- It is believed that this is just one of the many universes which have been created.

- In the Upanishads there are references to how balance is maintained through the vast and continuous sacrifice. The five elements – ether, air, water, earth and fire – are all engaged in continual sacrifice. The world of plants sacrifices itself to animals, animals to one another and to humans, and so on. So it is humans' self-sacrifice which sustains their children. In this way, there is a never-ending destruction and renewal of all life and matter. A verse in the Rig Veda describes the sacrifice of Purusha, the Cosmic Man, likening the elements of the sacrifice to the seasons (see the quote on the left).

At the end of the last age there was a great deluge which destroyed the universe. Brahma, the creator, prayed to Brahman to create a new universe. It is believed that when Brahma sleeps, then nothing exists. When he awakes then the world takes shape.

Creation in Buddhism

- Details as to how the universe came into being cannot be answered.
- The universe has always been in existence, and changing and developing.
- There is no belief in a creator being.

Buddhists do not believe that there was a creator god who brought the world into existence. Indeed, Buddha himself taught that endless discussions about when the universe began and when it might end are neither positive or helpful; far better to concentrate on leading a life that helps to move towards enlightenment and to nirvana.

The Big Bang Theory

Many people feel that this theory is a little more acceptable than creation to scientific thinking.

This theory, as its name suggests, states that everything began with a big bang. The dense matter that made up the universe began to expand about 15,000 million years ago, bursting out with great force and speed. Since then, the expansion has continued, with a gradual cooling down of the earth and other planets.

The knowledge we have of the universe seems to confirm this theory, as the stars in the universe are all burning masses, just like our sun. They also have planets grouped around them in galaxies, all moving apart and cooling down.

Whether this expanding continues for ever, or eventually begins contracting again until there is another big bang is uncertain, and people have differing views about it.

💡 Exam Tip

In answers explaining religious beliefs or teachings ensure that you give sufficient information to gain higher marks. You should always give at least **three** clear statements or explanations.

> St Thomas Aquinas believed:
> ❝Everything that happens has a cause. If we follow each cause back we come to a First Cause that started everything off. That First Cause is God.❞

> Professor J. Wickramasinghe stated:
> ❝The idea that life was put together by random shuffling is as ridiculous and improbable as the idea that a tornado blowing through a junk yard may assemble a Boeing 747. The aircraft had a creator and so has life.❞

Two important things to note about the Big Bang idea:

- It is only a theory, and some scientists do not accept some of the evidence and question its accuracy.

- There are some unanswerable questions about the theory, such as 'what caused the bang?' and 'where did the matter come from in the first place?'

Many Christians are happy to accept the principle of the Big Bang, and understand God as the cause of the Bang.

Some think it unnecessary to ask who caused it, but we should just acknowledge that it happened, and that the principle of cause and effect we now recognise in the world had come about through the processes following the explosion.

Only one of these moths is likely to survive in this environment.

> Did God really create humans?
> Or did he just begin the process?

> Are humans really unique?
> Or are they just evolved apes, and therefore just like any other animal?

The Theory of Evolution

Another scientific theory that raises questions about belief in creation is Darwin's theory of the origins of life – or evolution. During the nineteenth century, when investigating the distribution of animals in the islands of the Southern Hemisphere, Charles Darwin noticed how animals had adapted to changes in their environment. He was able to show clearly that changes in the physical make up of animals resulted from a process of natural selection. This was where the best and fittest survived and passed on their characteristics to a new generation.

It was this principle Darwin suggested in his book *The Origin of Species*, that over millions of years changes have been occurring, and the complex forms of life existing today are likely to have evolved from simpler and earlier forms of life.

To many, this raises doubts about God's role in creation, as it seems that species evolved from one thing to another over time in a process that happened through natural selection rather than divine intervention. The idea also suggests that human beings, rather than being created in God's image, had evolved from apes, and were merely a more complex and rational version.

On the other hand, many religious believers see no real conflict at all, as they either believe God established the process of natural selection as the means for life to evolve, or that evolution is a process that God is involved in from time to time so as to bring about a significant change or development.

It is important to note the following points about the theory of evolution:

● It is a theory, and has not been proved absolutely.

● It describes a process of development and adaptation within species – the question is still not completely clear about transformation from one species to another.

● It does not explain the origins of the first life forms.

● It does not explain the order in the universe, or the reason for 'natural laws' that exist within the universe.

Science and religion

All these issues raise questions about the relationship between science and religion.

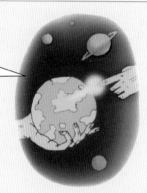

Are they complementary?

Science and religion do not go against each other; they answer different questions, and together give us a bigger picture.

Can a scientist be a Christian? Can a Christian accept scientific reasoning?

❛ I have faith in the Mathematics I teach, even though it is all based on unprovable axioms. I have a far more important faith ... in the living God ... (the reality of God's existence is a 'self-evident truth'). ❜

(Anne Sweeney, Lecturer in Mathematics)

Do they conflict?

❛ Science without religion is lame; religion without science is blind. ❜

(Albert Einstein)

❛ Science and religion seek to answer different questions. Science asks how things happen, religion asks why. Genesis is not there to give us strict, technical answers about how the universe began. It gives us the big answer that things exist because of God's will. One can perfectly well believe in the Big Bang but believe it as the will of God the creator. ❜

(John Polkinghorne, Professor of Mathematical Physics, University of Cambridge)

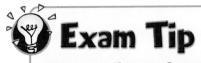 **Exam Tip**

How to do evaluative questions

Try to follow the simple guide below, and so make sure that you deal with all aspects of this type of question; you will then find you meet the criteria of the Levels of Response Grid for AO2 questions, as shown on page 124.

Select ...	... specialist language for the issue.	*Choose key terms that you need to use in your answer.*
What do you think and why?	Ask yourself, 'What is the statement saying?' and, 'What do I think about that?' Then write down your own thinking about the issue.	*Read it carefully, think about it sensibly, and write your own thinking clearly.*
Apply religious teaching or example.	Show how religious teaching affects the way you think, or give an example of something from religion that affects the answer you have offered.	*Make sure the links between religious beliefs, teachings and practice are clear.*
What's another point of view?	Think about other views – not necessarily just the opposite view! Comment on them sensitively, and acknowledge their contribution to the debate about the issue; show you understand the other view.	*Make sure you consider other views or ideas clearly and sensitively.*
Offer religious/moral teachings for the other point of view.	Make it clear how religious/moral teachings also affect the alternative view you have referred to. Show that alternative views are also based on what those people believe/value.	*Show clearly that religious beliefs, teachings and practice affect the views people have on the issue.*
Suggest how your response might impact ...	... on the individual and society when making your judgement. Top marks are only awarded to answers that make this impact clear.	*End with a clear conclusion about the impact of your answer or view on individuals and society.*

'Believing that the world was created is not in line with modern knowledge.' Do you agree? Give reasons or evidence for your answer, showing that you have thought of more than one point of view. You must refer to religious beliefs in your answer. [8]

Note how this answer uses the SWAWOS framework. Make sure you always use all of it.

Select specialist language
Key terms are used in the answer (the **bold** words).

What do you think and why?
A clear statement with reasons is given.

Apply religious teaching or example.
Clear references are made in the answer.

What's another point of view?
Other views are stated and commented on.

Offer religious/moral teachings for the other point of view.
This is clearly and simply done in the answer.

Suggest how your response might impact ...
There is clear reference to what results from the stated belief.

I do not agree with the statement, although I do understand why some people may make such statements.

The reason I disagree is that **religious views** about the **beginning of the universe** do not necessarily try to explain all the details of how the world began, but more the **purpose** and **reason** behind their existence. So, **Christians** who believe that **God created** the world are saying four key things: (1) that everything was created for a purpose; (2) that life's beginnings were not accidental; (3) that humans are different from animals; and (4) the world was basically good. To them, creation might be **evolution**, but it is God who is behind it all, and who gives purpose to existence.

Scientific views also try to explain how things began. To them, the 'answer' has to be scientific evidence, not belief. Science helps us to know a great deal about the universe. As knowledge progresses the theories are open to being re-written as new information or understanding becomes available. As such, they are not as certain as some would believe.

Some think that scientific knowledge of the world is more reliable than religious views on **creation**. So for them, science and modern technology raise serious questions about religious **creation stories** and beliefs.

However, I feel that **religion** and **science** are not in conflict. They are answering different kinds of questions, and both have something to offer to our wider understanding of the universe. Many **Buddhists** would argue that speculating over and over about where, when and how the universe began is pointless as it does not help people deal with their lives and how to live them now. So I think that believing the world was created is not out of step with modern knowledge. Believers in **creation** can have a real sense of **purpose** and **value** about life and what it means, and may live their lives in ways that make positive and worthwhile contributions to **humanity.**

Now do your own answer to the evaluation question using the **SWAWOS** framework.

Why should we care for the world?

Who Made a Mess?

Who made a mess of the planet
And what's that bad smell in the breeze?
Who punched a hole in the ozone
And who took an axe to my trees?

Who sprayed the garden with poison
While trying to scare off a fly?
Who streaked the water with oil slicks
And who let my fish choke and die?

Who tossed that junk in the river
And who stained the fresh air with fumes?
Who tore the fields with a digger
And who blocked my favourite views?

Who's going to tidy up later
And who's going to find what you've lost?
Who's going to say that they're sorry
And who's going to carry the cost?

(*Steve Turner*)

❝We are facing an environmental crisis. The planet is more threatened by the danger to its life systems than it has ever been through war.❞

(Maurice Strong Secretary General, United Nations Committee on Environment and Development)

Check it out

Always add examples

Environment

The natural world all about us – plants, insects, animals and humans which believers see as God's creation

The surroundings in which we live for which religions teach we are responsible

Some people have felt that to have 'dominion' over the world and animals allows them to exploit the world. All religions teach the sanctity of life, including that of animals.

For many years, humans have plundered the world and the environment, and are now beginning to recognise the importance of responsible management of the earth's *natural resources* and its environment.

NATURAL RESOURCES – a phrase that means the products that come from the earth: all the things that grow, and the things used for food such as fruits and vegetables, etc., the minerals in the ground, the soil and rocks too, and the water. All of these are the resources that exist in the world and on which humans rely a great deal.

Check it out

Always add examples

Dominion

Being in charge of the world for God

Having a form of control and responsibility which was given to humans by God

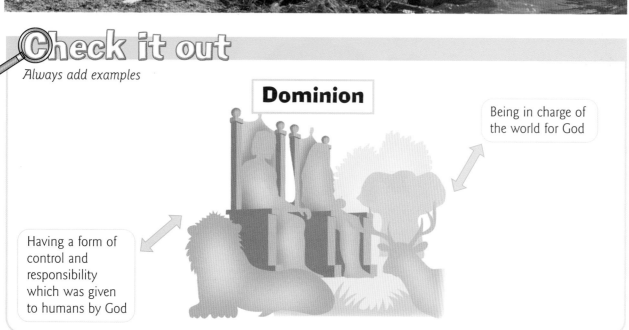

Christianity ✝

Christians would say that if humans learn to live sensibly and in true partnership with God and his creation, including animals, then they find nature itself responds and people come closer to God as they praise him for all he has provided.

Christians try to remind themselves that God did not only create the world in the beginning, but that his hand is still at work in the natural cycle of the world and its seasons.

So they remind themselves regularly, in worship and celebrations, of God's provision and their own responsibility too (for example, harvest thanksgiving; grace before meals).

There are many organisations and individuals who work to protect the earth and wellbeing of animals. Many humans, because of religious or moral teachings, feel they have a responsibility to care for the earth and all that lives in it. Many people feel they are partners with God in looking after the world.

Christians use the term stewardship to explain this responsibility.

Check it out

Always add examples

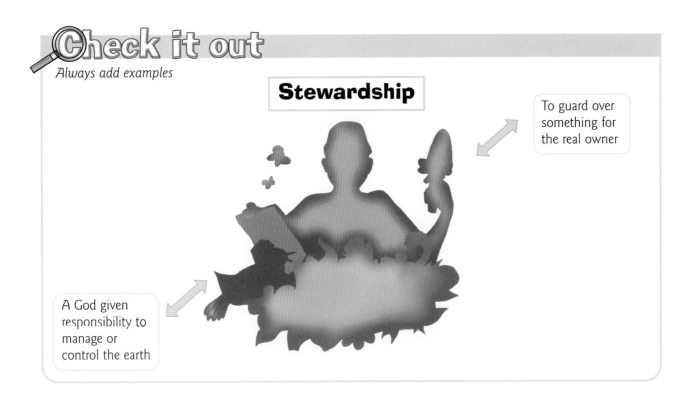

Stewardship

To guard over something for the real owner

A God given responsibility to manage or control the earth

An example of a Christian steward:

CHICO MENDES

Situation: In Brazil there had been environmental problems. Huge hardwood trees were being chopped down to make furniture and buildings. Mercury was being used to help separate gold from the land. This had another effect of polluting the water, and so killing the fish and anyone drinking the water. Rainforests were being burnt down to make space for crops and livestock. After three years the land had become exhausted, barren, and then abandoned. Many people living there just wanted the area to be left alone.

Who was Chico Mendes?

Chico was a leader of the rubber tappers. He had been a rubber tapper since the age of nine. As a rubber tapper he had not been able to go to school. Later in his life he organised the rubber tappers to defend their homes from cattle ranchers. From the 1970s he organised non-violent resistance to the exploitation of the forests. He found ways to use Amazonian resources to support the economic benefit for the local people and to protect the rainforest from logging and cattle ranching.

In 1988 he led a winning effort to stop cattle ranchers from deforesting an area the rubber tappers wanted to make into a reserve.

Chico was killed outside his house later that year by the son of a cattle rancher.

In his memory, the land he lived and died for – the 970,570,000 hectares – was named the Chico Mendes Extractive Reserve.

Look it up

www.chicomendes.com

Exam Tip

In some questions – especially about the environment – it may be possible to answer almost entirely by stating general ideas, rather than specific religious beliefs or teachings. It is possible for general ideas to be included, but the questions ask for descriptions or explanations of religious beliefs or teachings, so be sure to include them in your answer.

Q *Explain the teaching from two religious traditions about caring for the world and the environment.*   [6]

Look at the two answers below. Using the Levels of Response Grids on page 123, what marks would you give for each? State why. Identify the differences between them, and note what you need to do to ensure higher level marks in your own answers.

Answer A	Answer B
(i) Humans are responsible for caring for the world as it is them who pollute the environment. So they should clean it up, or they won't have a world to live in anyway. They have the power and the means to look after it, so they should. (ii) Hindus are very gentle people and they try not to harm other living things. So they often take more care about the world and the creatures in it – which others of us would do well to follow.	(i) Muslims believe that Allah made the world and all that is in it. Humans are the most important, and are believed to be khalifahs. As such they should use their talents and intelligence to look after the world and care for the environment. Muslims believe that people will be asked questions on judgement day about how much they have done for the world. (ii) Hindus believe that all living things should be respected. Each has an atman, a self or soul, and so their life is sacred and should not be harmed. They call this 'Ahimsa' – not harming living things, but having reverence for all life. Many Hindus are vegetarians as a result of these beliefs. However, because they believe life is sacred in this way, it means that they try to ensure they care for other living things, and not only not harm them, but help them to continue and to thrive.

Islam ☪

Muslims believe that Allah created, owns and sustains the world and all its creatures. The creation is considered as a whole, of which plants, animals and humans are a part. This is just like the *ummah* where all Muslim believers, irrespective of race, age or background, are seen as part of a whole. Every human is believed to have a special role as a *khalifah* to protect the environment.

> 'He has made you His ruling agents in the earth'
> (Surah 6:165)

UMMAH – the community of Muslim believers

KHALIFAH – agent or steward working for Allah

FITRAH – balance in the natural world

Adam's children are the limbs of
    one another
For in creation, they are from one
    substance
When times causes pain to one limb
The other limbs cannot rest
If you do not care for the afflictions
    of others
You do not deserve to be called a
    human being.

(*Verse from a poem by the Sufi poet, Sadi*)

The survival of the planet depends upon maintaining the natural *fitrah* and realising the interdependency on each other. There are many examples of where the earth has been damaged by deforestation and the extinction of species of animals. Muslims consider it a duty to use their skills to help keep the balance which Allah created.

In Islam, the more that one possesses, the more one should ensure its ethical use. This responsibility is so serious that on the Day of Judgement Muslims believe they will need to answer to Allah how they have treated the earth and all living creatures. The Prophet Muhammad set an example of the care that should be given to the natural world, showing kindness to animals is considered an important act. All animals and insects are part of Allah's creation – no matter how big or small! He often spoke of the importance of planting trees and gardens from which birds, animals and humans could benefit. There are many examples in the Hadith (Sayings of Muhammad) of how the Prophet avoided waste, was kind to animals, and respected the earth.

How the Prophet Muhammad showed the importance of all creation:	
In his sayings:	*In his actions:*
'The whole earth has been created a place of worship, pure and clean' (respect the earth) 'Live in this world as if you were going to live forever' (don't waste resources)	On a long journey, Muhammad and some travelling companions lit a fire to keep themselves warm. The Prophet then realised that nearby was an anthill, and the ants were running in the direction of the fire. Muhammad had the fire immediately extinguished. One day the Prophet passed by a camel that had been mistreated. He taught the listening people, 'Fear Allah in these beasts – ride them in good health and free them from work while they are still in good health.'

Interview with Safia, a Muslim

Safia is a sixteen-year-old Muslim girl living in Cardiff. She was born in England and is studying at school for her GCSEs. Safia is trying to convince her friend Helen to be more environmentally friendly.

Safia: Helen, you've left the taps on again! Have you any idea how much water you are wasting? Water is precious you know.

Helen: That's fine, coming from you. Have you ever thought how much water you waste getting washed before prayers?

Safia: It's called wudu, and we always make sure we only use the minimum. In fact, at the mosque, all the taps are controlled so that they only let a little water out. Prophet Muhammad said we must not waste water, even if we lived near a river. The teachers in the *madrassah* (mosque school) are always concerned about how we look after the environment. Last year, the mosque won a 'Cardiff in Bloom' competition for the care we took with our garden.

Helen: Why do you have a garden? At our church we have a graveyard. Does that count?

Safia: The Prophet Muhammad often spoke about the beauties of a garden. After a hard day at school, I like to go to the garden because it helps me remember that Allah is the creator, and that I have been given the responsibility to act as a *khalifah*, or guardian.

Helen: What do you mean 'guardian'? You're only sixteen! What can you do to help the world?

Safia: A lot! As a Muslim I have a commitment to the whole Muslim community – the *ummah*. It is a duty for me to make sure that I respect the environment and make sure I treat animals as a part of Allah's creation.

Helen: But how can you say that when you eat meat? If you cared for animals you would be a vegetarian.

Safia: Well, there are certain meats, such as pork, that I am not allowed to eat, but all the animals must be killed in the quickest and kindest way possible. We never take food for granted. When we fast during the month of Ramadan, it reminds us of how precious food is. After the fast we are always grateful for the food we believe Allah has provided.

Look it up

www.ifees.org.uk

Judaism

Jews believe they have a duty to look after the world which God has created, and which is only loaned to humans.

There are many ways Jews will carry out their responsibilities, but they can be summed up as:

- **T**hanksgiving
- **L**itter-free
- **C**oncern.

> The Earth is the Lord's and the fullness thereof.
>
> (Psalm 24:1)

Thanksgiving

There are many festivals in the Jewish calendar, and many of the celebrations concern thanking God for the environment.

Sukkot – This festival comes in the autumn months and many Jews build a *sukkah* in their garden or at their synagogue. This is a building like a booth in which, during the festival, some families will eat their meals or even sleep. The walls are made of canvas or thin board, and the roof will be made from leafy branches through which it will be possible to see the sky. Staying in the sukkah reminds people how they are dependent on God and his creation.

Tu B'Shevat – At this festival it is remembered how important trees are for all human existence. As part of the celebration young trees are often planted.

Litter-free

Jews believe it is important that there is no waste, and try to ensure that in their own lifestyle.

Concern

It is expected that animals will be treated with concern and compassion, as they too are part of God's creation. Most Jews do not agree with hunting, and care should be taken that when an animal is slaughtered it should be done as painlessly as possible.

Shocking abuse of chickens

On 8 September 2008, Let the Animals Live (Israel) fielded a shocking report about the slaughter of an entire coop of aged hens.

The hens were killed by electrocution. However, the machinery was not operating properly and caused dreadful suffering. Live birds were doomed to die of heat, dehydration, starvation – or to be crushed to death by the weight of dead chickens tossed into the container.

A Let the Animals Live spokeswoman commented that it was one of the worst cases she has encountered. Slaughter should be done as humanely as possible, to prevent animal suffering, she said.

The Jewish National Fund

Many Jewish homes and shops show their support of the environment by putting charity money in their blue Jewish National Fund collecting box. The first blue collecting boxes were used in 1904, and since then money raised in them has bought 12.5 per cent of all land in Israel.

Originally a large part of the funds was used to develop the land by planting trees. In recent times more attention is being given to the importance of providing water.

Look it up

www.jnf.co.uk

JNF WATER PROJECT IN ISRAEL

The project follows the JNF five-year Besor reservoir project in the Negev. With a capacity of 4 million cubic metres of water, it is the largest reservoir in the Middle East.

'Water is Israel's most vital resource, and the key to evenly distributing Israel's ever-growing population is to ensure there is a ready supply of it – for drinking and agriculture,' said JNF chief executive, Simon Winters.

Hinduism ॐ

ATMAN – self; usually refers to the real self, the soul

As Hindus believe that all living beings have *atman*, so they consider all life to be precious and sacred, and should not be harmed.

All animals are to be respected but special honour is given to the cow, who provides milk and butter, and works in the fields. The respect they give to the cow reflects their thankfulness to the earth.

This belief in non-violence is called *ahimsa*, and means 'to have reverence for all life'. Many Hindus show *ahimsa* by being vegetarians, and refusing to eat any part of an animal that has been slaughtered. Some Hindus also refuse to eat eggs, as they could become living beings.

For every hair on the body of a beast, the person who kills it without reason will be slaughtered in successive births.

(Manu 5, 38)

Vrindavan

Vrindavan lies 80 miles south of Delhi and is particularly important to may Hindus as it was here that Krishna was born and lived. By the 1980s most of the trees had been cut down, having an effect on the environment and animals.

With support from the World Wildlife Fund, the Vrindavan Forest Revival Project organised a major tree-planting programme, as well as educational projects. Recent developments have included the cleaning of the Yamuna River.

**Look it up**

www.mathura-vrindavan.com

THE VRINDAVAN DECLARATION

Nature enjoys being enjoyed, but reacts furiously to exploitation. Today's situation is caused by our separation from Krishna and his message of commitment. Let us act on his message to play, not to exploit.

Buddhism

As there is no traditional teaching about the creation of the world in Buddhism, there is no sense of the dominion of humans over the world, or any sense of the world (including animals) and humans being separate. Rather, humans are part of the whole universe, along with all other aspects that make it up.

Everything in the universe depends on everything else, so it is important for Buddhists to care for the world and the environment. If all forms of animal, human and plant life are dependent on each other for their existence, then it follows that caring for animals, other humans and the plant life of the world will all help to improve human life too.

This is seen as 'collective karma' – a term meaning that because humans live in the world, then they are responsible for its current condition (through their past actions) and can be responsible for its future condition (through their present actions). Therefore, activities that help to protect the environment, to renew damaged sites or areas, and to promote healthy, safe and sustainable environments and conditions will make a difference in the future.

In the same way, failing to take action, or activities that merely destroy or pollute the environment, will affect the future too – through leading to a still more polluted and neglected planet. The principle of *ahimsa* – that is harmlessness – is often thought to be about not harming other humans, or animals. But it also extends to not harming living things in general – the plants and other living entities of the natural world.

'Just as with her own life a mother shields from hurt her own, her only, child – let all embracing thoughts for all that lives be thine, – an all-embracing love for all the universe in all its heights and depths and breadth . . .'

(Sutta Nipata)

Green Pagodas Project

This project is led by the Association of Buddhists for the Environment (ABE), an organisation bringing together the Buddhist monks from the 23 provinces of Cambodia, and exists to help the community of Buddhist monks and nuns to work together and protect the environment.

It was founded in March 2005, and its main aim is to promote a cleaner and healthier environment, and the preservation of the natural resources of forestry, wildlife and aquatic resources.

By training the monks and nuns to create models of good practice within their temples and grounds, the expectation is that the monks can encourage the locals by sharing their experiences and good practices with the communities around them, and train them to improve the community environment too.

ABE has established a partnership with UNESCO, and has the support of the Conservation International organisation.

Among the activities to raise awareness, Buddhist monks from temples take 'spiritual walks' (*dhammyietra*) to inspire the local communities to think about protecting their environment. They also carry out tree ordination ceremonies, to help people to think about the importance of protecting the forest systems, and being careful and respectful of natural resources.

They ensure that 'environmentally friendly' practices are being installed in the temples so that local people can see the monks are putting into practice the things they are encouraging others to do. Some of the projects temples have engaged in are:

- Managing well-digging projects to improve water provision
- Producing compost fertilisers
- Planting and caring for trees
- Clearing the pagodas' grounds
- Creating model fruit and vegetable gardens
- Improving cooking stoves
- Caring for local wildlife.

Look it up
www.sanghanetwork.org

A more local UK project is the Jamyang Buddhist Garden of Contemplation, which was created in the derelict buildings of the Elephant and Castle courthouse in south London.

The courthouse buildings had been left derelict for five years, and a local Buddhist group, under the direction of Alison Murdoch, decided to buy the site and turn it into a garden of contemplation – as well as a centre offering meditation, meeting rooms, a counselling service and a vegetarian café.

Sikhism

Sikhs believe that God created the world and everything in it, not in just a past activity, but in an ongoing and continual process.

Therefore Sikhs should show respect towards nature and all that God provides, and also be grateful for all that humans gain from the natural world. Sikhs respect all life forms, human, animal or other, because they also recognise that the divine inner spark is in all beings.

In the stories of the Gurus are many examples of them showing kindness and respect towards animals and birds, trees and vegetation, and towards mountains, rivers and the sky.

Sikhs also see human beings as the 'custodians' – the ones who look after or are guardians of the world and all that is in it. That is not to say that humans should be 'masters' over the world and its creatures, for it is learning to control oneself that is the key; but Sikhs long for a life that is simple and free from waste and destruction. For many Sikhs – but not all – these beliefs lead also to being vegetarian.

Sikhism has followed 300-year cycles, and the current cycle, which began in 1999, is labelled the *Cycle of Creation*. As a result, there has been a huge increase in the number of environmental projects and schemes by Sikhs and Sikh organisations.

> 'The universe comes into being by God's Will.'
>
> (Guru Nanak – Adi Granth 1)
>
> 'The Lord who created the world is Lord of all, Whose form is subtle, whose name is the Bright One, and whose image is in all minds. He continues to give us our daily bread which never fails.'
>
> (Guru Granth Sahib)

Khalsa Wood Project

This project is an example of such a scheme. British Sikhs planted a special woodland on the outskirts of Nottingham in 1999, and now it is a quiet place, used for walks, picnics, celebrations and meditations. It is known as Khalsa Wood, and is within Bestwood Country Park.

At first, 300 oak trees were planted, in memory of the 300th anniversary of Vaisakhi. Fruit trees – apple, pear and plum – have also been planted, and a specially carved gateway has been erected, largely through the activities of the Sikh Youth Group in the local community.

Other groups and people use the wood too, and people of all ages use the site. There are research and investigation activities available, live performances take place too; there are trails and interpretive materials, exhibitions and multilingual information leaflets.

Look it up

www.lhi.org.uk/docs/Sikhusm_and_KhalsaWood_project.pdf

www.arcworld.org/news.asp?pageID=232

Exam Tip

Within many units you will be expected to know about the **impact** of the work of one individual or agency. In this unit you will be expected to have a knowledge and understanding of one agency or individual that has used their particular talents to help care for the environment. There are a number of questions you should ask yourself – these are shown below.

Who Should I Choose?

The person or agency you refer to may be local, national or international. It may be someone you have studied as a class or that you have a particular interest in.

Remember the Specification requires your study to be from particular faith beliefs. You must make sure the person/agency you have chosen is from one of the religions you are studying.

What Do I Need To Know?

You will be expected to show in your answer what the person or agency:

1 does to care for the earth;

2 why they have this concern, and

3 what their religious inspirations are.

You do not need to know a list of dates or family details. Your answers should show that you have an understanding of the IMPACT of their work.

Where Will I Get My Information From?

You may take your particular study as a class lesson or be expected to conduct your own research. The amount of detail you need to know depends upon whether you are using the information to answer an exam question or part of a piece of coursework. Whichever, you should refer to **as wide a range as possible**.

Websites – many agencies and individuals have informative websites. You will find some useful examples in the 'Look it up' boxes in this book.

Newspapers – you may find relevant information in daily newspapers. Many religions have their own newspapers or magazines, such us: *Catholic Herald; Jewish Chronicle; Q News.*

Publicity materials – often an agency will produce DVDs or booklets describing the work they do and any current events.

Interviews – if a local person or agency is your focus, then you may be able to conduct your own interview.

Range of books – do not rely on just one book; use a number of them to get a wider picture.

Task

- Select one person or agency who has used their talents to care for the environment. Then fill in the following framework. **Remember to be precise. The whole answer should illustrate the IMPACT of their work.**

I dentify   the correct name of the person or agency.

M ention   the religious tradition to which they belong.

P récis   the context in which the person or agency is working.

A cknowledge   some of the main aspects of their work.

C onsider   how their work demonstrates the teachings of the religion to which they belong.

T ell   of specific examples of the long- and short-term projects.

TEST IT OUT

Here is a typical set of examination questions for this unit.

Write out answers to them, trying to take account of the Exam Tips and information you have been given.

(a) *Explain what religious believers mean by 'dominion'.*   [2]

(b) *Explain how religious believers feel we should use our talents.*   [4]

(c) *'Life has no built-in purpose; you make it yourself.'*
Give two reasons why a religious believer might agree or disagree with this statement.   [4]

(d) *Explain using **two** different religious traditions the teachings about creation.*   [6]

(e) *'The world is there for us humans to enjoy; that's all that matters.'*
Do you agree? Give reasons or evidence for your answer, showing that you have thought of more than one point of view. You must include reference to religious beliefs in your answer.   [8]

2 Relationships

The Big Picture

What is love?

What is the role and purpose of sex?

Whose decision is it to use contraception?

Is marriage out of date?

What commitments and responsibilities do we have towards each other?

How important is the family?

Is it necessary to marry in a place of worship?

Should people be allowed to remarry?

Should it be in a religious building?

Should same-sex marriages be allowed in a place of worship?

Why do marriages succeed and fail?

Questions to ask

Key concepts to think about ▼

COMMITMENT

CHASTITY

CONFLICT

♥ LOVE

RECONCILIATION

RESPONSIBILITIES

Religious teachings to explore

- Adultery and extra-marital sex
- Sex before marriage
  - Pre-marital relationships
  - Colibacy
  - Contraception
  - Sex as a gift from God
- Cohabitation
- Marriage
  - Courtship
  - Religious marriage services
  - Marriage vows and the meaning of marriage
- Divorce
- Remarriage
- Same-sex relationships

Check it out

The definitions in these boxes in this chapter are basic outlines only; always add an appropriate example in your explanation, and remember the context is religious believers.

What commitments and responsibilities do we have?

We have many different types of relationships with other people.

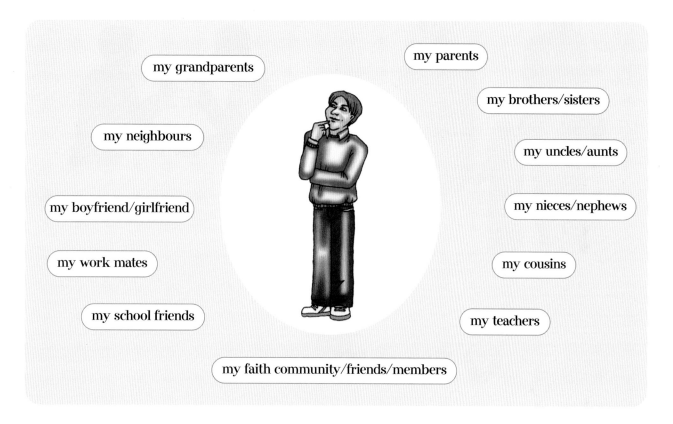

- my grandparents
- my parents
- my brothers/sisters
- my neighbours
- my uncles/aunts
- my boyfriend/girlfriend
- my nieces/nephews
- my work mates
- my cousins
- my school friends
- my teachers
- my faith community/friends/members

The relationships are all different, and we respond differently to each of the people.

- **What do you think your responsibilities are to:**
  a) your parents
  b) your relatives
  c) your friends
  d) your neighbours?

- Choose two or three of the above, and write down what kind of **commitments** you make to those people.

Check it out

Always add examples

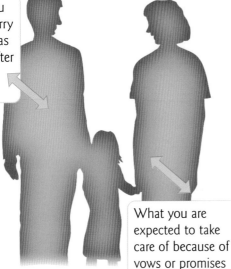

Responsibilities

Duties you should carry out such as looking after family members

What you are expected to take care of because of vows or promises you have made

Check it out

Always add examples

Commitment

Being devoted towards someone or something. This may be shown by being faithful to them

Making and keeping a promise such as wedding vows

Exam Tip

When giving an answer that requires an explanation of a key term always be precise but remember to explain, not just state. Where possible relate your answer to what religious believers might say.

> **Q** *Explain what religious believers mean by commitment in marriage.* [2]

Look at the two answers below and you will see a full answer and a part answer.

Answer A	Answer B
Devotion	Being completely devoted to each other and keeping the wedding vows that you made.

What is 'love'?

Most people develop special relationships with particular individuals.

Friends – these may be people of either sex with whom we have a lot in common, and we like to spend time with them.

Boyfriend/Girlfriend – this is a particular person for whom we develop a very close friendship.

Some people would describe their feelings with the word 'love'.

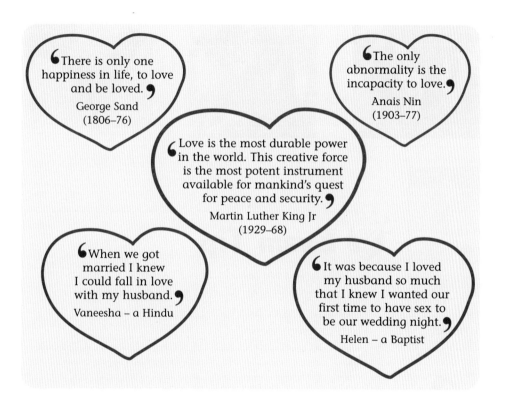

> There is only one happiness in life, to love and be loved.
> George Sand (1806–76)

> The only abnormality is the incapacity to love.
> Anais Nin (1903–77)

> Love is the most durable power in the world. This creative force is the most potent instrument available for mankind's quest for peace and security.
> Martin Luther King Jr (1929–68)

> When we got married I knew I could fall in love with my husband.
> Vaneesha – a Hindu

> It was because I loved my husband so much that I knew I wanted our first time to have sex to be our wedding night.
> Helen – a Baptist

Check it out

Always add examples

Love

To have a deep affection for someone and express it through your actions and words

It can often include a relationship where there is commitment between people

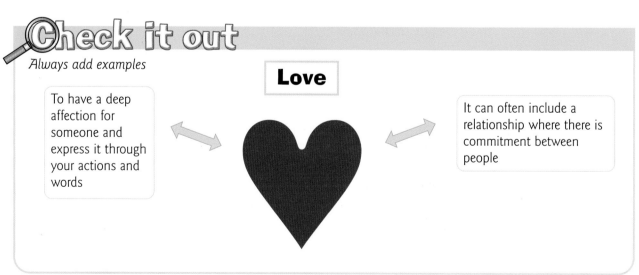

In the Greek of the New Testament, there are four words used to describe the one English word 'love':

στοργη (storge)	φιλια (philia)	ερος (eros)	αγαπη (agape)
Affection for things and animals. Sometimes described as 'sentimental love'.	Love of friends and family; a stronger bond between people.	Sexual love; physical love between two people, usually of the opposite sex.	Unconditional love, given freely and unreservedly.

Task

- How would you explain the difference in the love that you show for each of the following:

  a) your pet dog or cat
  b) your brother or sister
  c) your boyfriend/girlfriend?

Exam Tip

When you are asked to give two reasons make sure they are different. Many candidates do not gain full marks because they repeat the same examples in different words.

 Q 'Sex before marriage harms no one.'
Give **two** reasons why a religious believer might agree or disagree with this statement. [4]

Look at the two answers below. Which do you think was given two marks? How would you change the two-mark answer to get four marks?

Answer A	Answer B
Many Christians may disagree as sex is considered as a gift from God and should therefore take place within marriage. Sex is something special that should be kept for marriage.	Many Christians may disagree as sex is considered as a gift from God and should therefore take place within marriage. Most religious believers would say that sex should only take place in a loving and committed relationship so people aren't devalued.

What about sex?

Sex is a natural part of life. In fact many religions, such as Christianity see sex as a gift from God, and a joy to humanity. The sex drive is very strong, and so needs to be checked or controlled. The problem is that sex, like many things, can become a preoccupation, and something that leads to using or abusing others – a breaking of our responsibilities and commitments to them.

Before contraceptives were invented and available, it was true to say that chastity was the safest and only way to prevent unwanted pregnancies.

Check it out

Always add examples

Chastity

Not having any sexual relationships before marriage as sex is seen as sacred

Keeping oneself from sexual activity until married to someone as sex is seen as a gift from God

It's only natural

Within many religions, finding a partner is considered the natural state.

Most religions have teachings about marriage and sex before marriage. Believers from each tradition will refer to these teachings when making their decisions about personal relationships.

Christianity

- Marriage begins the special relationship between two people.

- The couple will usually be in love when they marry, but expect to develop that love.

- Marriage consists of one man to one woman at any one time.

- Considered a sacrament – a relationship in which God himself is involved.

- Sex should generally take place within marriage.

- Sex is a gift from God, and is holy and sacred; it is special and should be reserved between just two people at any one time/period in one's life.

- Casual sex or promiscuity is seen as devaluing both people and sex, and therefore is unacceptable.

- Bringing up children is an important part of marriage.

- There are different attitudes to same-sex marriages within Christianity.

- The Roman Catholic Church teaches that marriage is a faithful and exclusive union between man and woman.

- In the Anglican Church many clergy bless the same-sex couple although there is no actual authorised ceremony.

- Quakers have been welcoming same-sex unions for over 20 years.

Judaism

- Marriage begins the contract between two people with God's blessing.

- The couple will usually be in love when they marry, but expect that love to develop.

- Marriage consists of one man to one woman at any one time.

- Just like Adam and Eve, the couple should be a support for each other.

- Sex is expected only to take place within marriage.

- Sex is seen as one of the three stages of marriage – betrothal/contract/consummation.

- Bringing up children is an important part of marriage.

- There are different attitudes to same-sex marriages within Judaism.

- Liberal Jews support gay and lesbian rights, including same-sex marriages.

- Orthodox Judaism does not allow same-sex marriage.

Islam

- Marriage begins the relationship between two extended families, not just two individuals.

- Marriage is a social contract which has Allah's sanction.

- It is not a sacrament but a legal binding contract between man and woman.

- Sex should only happen within marriage.

- Couples are expected to meet each other's needs.

- Sex is considered an act of worship.

- Bringing up children is an important part of marriage.

- Polygamy (marriage of a man to more than one wife) is allowed in exceptional circumstances, and when the law of the land allows.

- Same-sex marriage is not allowed in Islam.

Hinduism

- Within the system of *varnashramadharma* the students must exercise chastity until the end of their studies.

- Marriage consists of one man to one woman.

- Marriage begins the relationship between two extended families, not just the individuals.

- Considered a sacrament – *samskara*.

- Begins the householder stage, and a new set of duties.

- Usually love is expected to grow and develop.

- Sex should only happen with marriage.

- *Kama* (sensual pleasure) is one of the four Hindu aims of life.

- Bringing up children is an important part of marriage.

- The differing interpretations of Hindu teachings mean that there is no official view on same-sex marriages.

Buddhism

- Buddhist monks and nuns should be celibate so that they can channel their energies into religious work.

- Theravada Buddhists believe that the celibate life that monks and nuns live is important for enlightenment.

- Mahayana Buddhists believe that married couples can also be enlightened.

- Sex must be controlled so that no suffering is caused.

- There is no official view of same-sex marriages. Some Buddhists consider it important to be tolerant of different lifestyles. Cambodia and Thailand, which have a large number of Buddhists, do not allow same-sex marriages.

Sikhism

- Sex should only be within marriage and it is expected that couples will have children.

- The wearing of the kachs by both sexes is a reminder of the need for chastity and faithfulness in marriage.

- Lust is one of five evil passions.

- The Guru Granth Sahib does not mention homosexuality.

Some people choose a *celibate* lifestyle. Sometimes this choice has been made to allow people to dedicate their lives to serving God. Those taking Holy Orders in the Roman Catholic Church are expected to remain celibate.

CELIBACY – deciding never to have a sexual relationship

Exam Tip

Many religious traditions may seem to have the same beliefs or practices, but is this really so? Make sure you know the differences in beliefs/practices and religious language of the two traditions you are studying.

Q *Explain from **two** different religious traditions why believers choose to marry.* [6]

Task

● **Correct this answer.**

> In my two religions, the couples get married because they love each other. They often want to have children. They believe sex should happen in marriage as it is a gift from God and they want to live happily ever after.

Religious traditions believe making sex something special within only a marriage relationship is not a negative thing, but is actually very positive.

Celebrates the JOY of sex	It is a celebration of the joy of sex as a mutual partnership – a complete giving of oneself totally and personally to another.
Highlights the RESPONSIBILITY	It is a highlighting of responsibility towards another person – a thinking about them and their needs, not just a satisfying of one's own needs.
States the place of COMMITMENT	It is a stating of the importance of commitment in their relationship – a willingness to spend the rest of one's life with someone you love.
Adds a SPIRITUAL DIMENSION	It is an enhancing of the relationship by including a religious and spiritual dimension – an understanding that the sexual relationship is not just physical uniting, but a spiritual and religious experience too.
Strengthens the legal side or CONTRACT	It strengthens the relationship as it becomes part of a legal and social joining of two lives – and ensures that both partners have clear rights should things go wrong.

SELENA GOMEZ: 'I WILL STAY CELIBATE UNTIL MARRIAGE'

Disney Star Selena Gomez has stated that she won't have sex before marriage. She has asked her father to buy her a promise ring so that she can make her virginity official. She said, 'He went to the church and got the ring blessed. I am going to keep my promise to the family and to God.'

The True Love Waits International movement involves many young people pledging themselves to be chaste until marriage.

Look it up

Christian teaching about adultery and extra-marital sex:

- Marriage is sexually exclusive – sex should not be shared with anyone else (the special relationship – or 'oneness' – is destroyed).

- The Ten Commandments and teaching of Jesus forbid it.

- It is harmful to the special relationship of marriage.

- The family can be harmed.

- A partner feels cheated, betrayed, or rejected.

- It is wrong because God himself is involved in the marriage (sacrament).

Hindu teaching about adultery and extra-marital sex:

- Marriage is a religious duty – a *samskara* – so the ideals of it are too, and will produce good *karma*.

- Hindu scriptures and society approve only of sex within marriage, and so chastity is encouraged prior to marriage, and fidelity within marriage.

- A vow or promise of faithfulness is made in the seventh step of the ceremony, and is seen as a lifelong commitment.

- Faithfulness to one's partner in marriage is depicted by Sita in the Ramayana.

- The *yamas* (five abstentions) and *niyamas* (five observances) preclude adultery: *yama* – lying, lust, greed; *niyama* – purity, patience, contentment.

Islamic teaching about adultery and extra-marital sex:

- Sex outside of marriage is generally strongly disapproved of.

- Sexual desires are to be satisfied, but only in the context of marriage.

- The ideal is a lifelong union based on trust, morality and devotion.

- Vows promising to be faithful are exchanged in the marriage ceremony.

- Adultery is seen as harmful socially, so against the unity and peace of the *ummah*.

- Adultery is seen as a form of theft of the worst possible sort: *'Have nothing to do with adultery, for it is a shameful thing and an evil opening the way to other evils'* (Surah 17:32).

Jewish teaching about adultery and extra-marital sex:

- The Ten Commandments specifically forbid adultery *'You shall not commit adultery'* (Exodus 20:13).

- Sex is only acceptable within marriage – a stable relationship between one man and one woman.

- *Halakhah* (code of conduct) emphasises that a husband should be sexually considerate towards his wife; and this precludes disloyalty sexually.

- Men and women are most fulfilled through marriage, which is referred to as '*kiddushim*' (sanctified).

Buddhist teaching about adultery and extra-marital sex:

- The middle way is the important path between indulgence and deprivation.

- Usually adultery causes suffering (*dukkha*) by someone and so should be avoided.

- The five precepts stress the importance of right intention and not causing harm towards others.

Sikh teaching about adultery and extra-marital sex:

- The only correct place for sex is within marriage.

- The *izzat* or honour of a Sikh family is very important.

- Lust is considered as one of the five evil passions.

- The Guru Granth Sahib teaches: 'Do not cast your eyes on the beauty of another's wife' (274).

Acrostics are often a good way of remembering key information, and for revising. Read the acrostic below, and then complete one for the key concept of Commitment.

Against the Ten Commandments

Damages lives

Undermines marriage

Lets others down

Trust is broken

Ends family security

Relationships harmed

You'd best avoid it!

 Task

• **Answer this question.**

Q *'People who marry as virgins will have a stronger bond of trust and commitment.' Do you agree? Give reasons or evidence for your answer, showing that you have thought about more than one point of view. You must include reference to religious beliefs in your answer.* [8]

Remember to use the SWAWOS framework (page 18).

So what happens?

If sex is to be kept until marriage, then marriage is being seen as a special event, and most religions have views about and ceremonies for marriage.

But marriage is by no means the only possibility:

I just want to live with my boyfriend, and hope that one day we could even marry! Why shouldn't we — we love each other totally.

We think marriage is an out-of-date institution; we cohabit and have a contract so we each know exactly our rights and responsibilities. We spent some time living together first, as a trial — to see if we got along together — and then drew up a proper contract.

I will never marry — but for just personal reasons. I do not want to be tied to a relationship nor do I want to have children.

I will never marry or have sexual relationships, as I have taken a religious vow of celibacy. I am 'married' to my calling to serve God.

My religion allows me to marry more than one wife — as long as I treat them both fairly, and love them — which I do.

2

Christian Marriage Ceremony

Religious marriage ceremonies

Remember, within all religious traditions, couples, with their families, will choose the actual content of their marriage ceremony.

E.g. A favourite hymn for weddings:
*O Perfect Love, all human
thought transcending,
Lowly we kneel in prayer
before Your throne,
That theirs may be the love
which knows no ending,
Whom You for evermore now join as one.*

'I, N, take you N, to be my
[husband/wife], to have and to
hold from this day forward; for
better, for worse, for richer, for
poorer, in sickness and in
health. To love and to cherish
till death do us part …'

'Love is patient and kind.
Love is not jealous, it does
not boast, and it is not proud.
Love is not rude, is not
selfish, and does not become
angry easily … Love always
trusts, always hopes, and
always continues strong.
Love never ends.'
(1 Cor: 13:4–8)

*Hymn
Purpose explained
Ask for impediments
Taking of vows
(with witnesses)
Exchanging rings
Pronounce union
Hymn
Bible reading
Sermon or talk
Prayers
Signing register
'Marching out'
Photos and reception*

The purposes of marriage are
clearly stated at the start of the
service. (Look these up in a
Prayer Book.)

The minister asks if anyone
knows any reason why the
couple should not be married.

The words recited by the bride and
groom as they give rings to each
other, explaining that the ring (a
circle without a beginning or end) is
a symbol of their never-ending love.

'I now pronounce you husband
and wife. Whom God has joined
let no man separate.'

The bride and groom, their parents,
and two witnesses all sign – to show
all was done legally and willingly.

To remind the couple of the
importance of their vows, and
of the sacredness of their new
life together and with God.

The party and celebration is a way of
marking this very special event for
the couple and their families.

Christianity ✝

Before a Christian marriage takes place there is
likely to be a lot of preparation for the big day:
arrangements for the service, the bride's and
bridesmaids' dresses, the flowers, and of course
the reception afterwards. The ceremony itself
will usually take place in a church or chapel,
because for believing Christians, marriage is a
sacrament, and there are religious elements that
they would want in their special day. For others,
marriage in a church is mainly for the setting,
and sometimes marriages are arranged in a
registry office, a hotel, or some other place.

Hinduism ॐ

Before a Hindu wedding takes place there will
have been much preparation. Parents and the
extended family will have assisted by searching
for suitable partners. The families will then
have arranged for the couple to have supervised
meetings after which they will decide whether
to continue the relationship or not. If the
couple feel the relationship is promising then
they will consult a priest who will look at their
horoscopes to see if they are compatible.

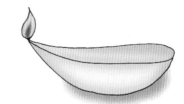

The process is often called an 'arranged marriage' but most Hindus would prefer to call it an 'assisted marriage'. Within the majority of families today, the couple themselves take a lead role in the arrangements with the family assisting or supporting the proceedings.

The wedding ceremony itself is considered by many Hindus to be one of the *samskaras* or rites of passage which begins a new stage of life. The ceremony itself can take place in a hall or *mandir*. Often a decorated *mandir* or canopy is erected under which the ceremony will take place. There are many important and symbolic aspects of the ceremony. For example, offerings to Ganesha – who it is believed can remove obstacles that can be put in the way of a marriage. A *havan* (fire) is lit and offerings of incense sprinkled into the flames. Agreement of the couple is asked for. The bride's scarf is tied to the groom's and they circle the fire. The bride places her toe on a stone to show her obedience and loyalty to her husband. Seven steps are taken around the fire for food, strength, wealth, happiness, children, long wedded life, and unity. During the ceremony, commitments to *dharma* (religious duty), *artha* (economic development) and *kama* (sense of enjoyment) will be made.

Islam

Before a Muslim marriage takes place there will have been much preparation. Within Islam it is believed important to allow the whole family to assist with the finding of the right partner. This is a practice which is often referred to as arranged or assisted marriages. This will include parents searching for a suitable partner which may then lead to the prospective couple meeting. From the meeting the couple will consider whether to continue with the relationship or to decide they are not compatible.

If they decide to continue, the *mahr* or dowry is arranged. This is the payment of an agreed sum of money to the wife. The money belongs to the wife, and is hers to keep should they later decide to divorce.

The ceremony, which means the couple are married under Islamic law, is called the *Nikah*, and may take place at home, in the mosque or anywhere else where the witnesses (often including an *imam* or leader) are present. The bride does not have to be present, but must send witnesses. Usually the ceremony will include:

- Recitation of *ayahs* (units of surahs from the Qur'an)
- Agreement to the *mahr* in front of witnesses
- Exchange of vows
- Signing the contract.

Exam Tip

Always include specific religious content and language in your answers even if it seems easier to write about more general cultural traditions.

Judaism

The marriage ceremony will usually be held in a synagogue, but can also take place in the open air. The format will differ depending upon whether the bride and groom are Liberal, Reform, or Orthodox Jews. The ceremony can take place on any day except *Shabbat* and festivals. Often there will have been a lot of preparation before:

- Lessons with the rabbi, to help the couple understand the importance of marriage.
- Fasting before the ceremony to help prepare the couple for a solemn time.

The ceremony is held under a *chuppah* (canopy) – which is often decorated with flowers – and supported by four poles. The groom and bride stand under the chuppah with other close relatives joining them during the service.

There are many important aspects of the ceremony which normally include the following:

- Blessings of wine and marriage
- Exchange of rings
- Music from the choir
- Sermon from the rabbi
- Signing the *ketubah* or marriage document
- Final seven blessings
- Breaking of the wine glass, to symbolise the fragility of marriage and the destruction of the Temple.

Buddhism

There are no specific religious marriage ceremonies in Buddhism. Buddhists would usually follow the customs of the country in which they live.

By many it is considered a family celebration at which the *sangha* (community) chant texts of blessing. Vows are sometimes made, which show the importance of marriage and the responsibilities of family members.

Sikhism

Usually the families will play a role in selecting the partners because marriage is considered as a union of two families. There is no tradition of arranged marriages. Before the wedding the bride's family and relatives will meet to have a celebration including present giving and henna painting.

The marriage service is called the *anand karaj*, which means 'ceremony of happiness'. The ceremony takes place in front of the Guru Granth Sahib and the bride's father puts a garland of flowers on it. The ceremony begins with prayers and readings. The bride is given the end of the bridegroom's scarf to hold symbolising being joined as husband and wife. Any Sikh can conduct the service as long as they have been chosen by the parents. The ideal marriage is to bring two souls together so they become one. The Guru Granth Sahib teaches, 'Only they who have one spirit in two bodies can be called husband and wife.' God sees and blesses marriage and during the reading of the *Lavan* (marriage hymn) mention is made of the soul's progression towards union with God. During this reading the bride and groom walk around the Guru Granth Sahib four times before they are married.

> **Q** *Explain from **two** different religious traditions the most important features of a marriage ceremony.* [6]

Look at the answer below. It has been given a Level 2 and 2 marks. How would you change it to give it a Level 4 and 6 mark (See Levels of Response grid on page 123)? The words below will help you with the answer: *vow, church, congregation, Bible, prayers, register.*

Answer

(i) The main part of the ceremony would be when the couple say the promises in their special place in front of all the people. The bride wears white and the man will normally wear a suit. All the people will say special things together. They will then be announced man and wife.

(ii) The main part is the promises made and the exchange of rings in a sacred place. The couple are told how sacred marriage is and its importance for the whole of their lives.

Same-sex marriages

Male Priests Marry in Anglican Church's First Gay 'wedding'

Although some clergy have carried out 'blessing ceremonies' for homosexual couples in the past, this was the first time a vicar has performed a 'wedding ceremony' using a traditional marriage liturgy, with readings, hymns and a Eucharist. The Archbishop of Uganda said the ceremony was 'blasphemous'.

The couple, the Rev Peter Cowell and the Rev Dr David Lord, had registered their civil partnership before the ceremony.

The service began with 'Dearly beloved, we are gathered here in the sight of God to join these men in a holy covenant of love and fidelity. Such a covenant shows us the mystery of the union between God and God's people and between Christ and the Church.' In the vows, Mr Cowell and Dr Lord pledged to 'hold from this day forward, for better for worse, for richer for poorer, in sickness and in health, to love and to cherish, till death us do part.'

Task

- From the article above, what are two main reasons for and against the blessing in the church?

What about the family?

For many couples, an important part of getting married is the possibility of having children. This also means that couples will need to plan their family, and consider when to have children, and how many to have.

Christianity ✝

There are varying views about family planning within Christianity. Some Christians say that contraception is acceptable, provided that:

- Sex is within a marriage (or permanent relationship).

- Both partners agree to using contraception, and which kind to use.

This view is based on the belief that in family life, quality is the most important thing.

Others, however, like some Roman Catholics, feel strongly that artificial methods of contraception are unacceptable. They would follow the rulings of the declaration of Pope Paul VI in *Humanae Vitae* that:

- Sexual intercourse should strengthen the bond between husband and wife.

- Sexual intercourse should always be open to the possibility of creating new life.

As a result, they believe that couples should only use natural methods of family planning, such as the rhythm method, and that the sexual act is a total self-giving of two people to each other in love.

I think we should plan what children we have, and not have them straight away.

I know that you are thinking about your career, but is it OK to use contraception? It's preventing a life from being born.

I know, but surely it is better to plan carefully, and know that you want and are ready for a child. God would want that. Do you remember those Bible Study sessions we had, when we discussed family planning?

Yes. But the Bible does not have anything to say about contraception. Let's see, wasn't there something helpful in this book about general Christian principles?

OK, so we will use contraception for a while, and then have our children in a year or so. Is that all right with you?

Yes. Our children must be wanted and well as loved, and we can make sure we are ready and able to look after them too.

Hinduism ॐ

For some Hindus contraception is allowed, but for others it is considered as contrary to the practice of *ahimsa* (non-violence). Often social and economic factors are considered more influential than religious issues. Many couples do not believe that children should be conceived out of lust, and take part in the *garbhadhan samskara* when prayers are said to purify the womb and prepare the way for the soul of a new child to enter.

Islam ☪

Attitudes to contraception may differ according to a couple's interpretation of Islamic tradition; however it should never be used to encourage promiscuity. Some couples do use artificial methods of contraception. Forms such as the pill and condom are generally considered more acceptable than those which are difficult to reverse, such as vasectomy.

Judaism 🕎

The procreation of children is believed to be part of the divine intention. In the book of Isaiah it states then when God made the world, 'he formed it to be inhabited' (Isaiah 45:18).

Many Jews consider large families to be a blessing from God. There are a variety of opinions over whether it is acceptable to use contraceptives or not. Oral contraceptives are considered preferable to those forms of contraception which interfere with intercourse and where the male seed is destroyed. Condoms are generally considered as unacceptable as they prevent the true bonding of bodies.

Buddhism ☸

Usually it is believed that it is up to a married couple whether they have children. Before a couple considers contraception they must be sure that their actions follow the precept to not take life. Buddhists would consider the reason why a couple want to use contraception, for example, is the mother's life at risk? The responsibility of whether to use contraception must be considered against the precepts.

Sikhism ☬

Contraceptives are not forbidden but there is often an expectation that married couples will have children.

Happily ever after?

Why do some marriages fail?

Living with other people is not an easy thing, and being married to a person, and experiencing everything in life with that partner means that both people have to learn to give and take, and to work at making their relationship a happy and lasting one.

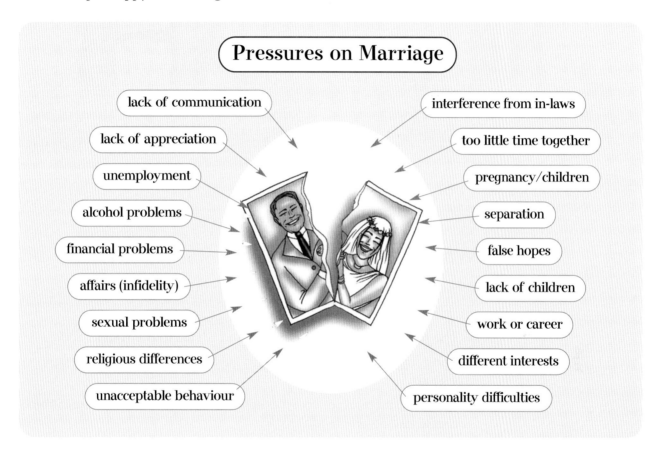

Pressures on Marriage

- lack of communication
- lack of appreciation
- unemployment
- alcohol problems
- financial problems
- affairs (infidelity)
- sexual problems
- religious differences
- unacceptable behaviour
- interference from in-laws
- too little time together
- pregnancy/children
- separation
- false hopes
- lack of children
- work or career
- different interests
- personality difficulties

Because of all these pressures, sometimes conflict comes into marriage and the family. When this happens, there needs to be some reconciliation if the couple and family are to get along together, and build up their relationship.

Task

- Can you think of other pressures on marriage?
- Choose three and say how religious believers could help someone cope with them.

Always add examples

Conflict

Working against each other rather than together in unity

Clashes and breakdown of relationships. Faith communities may help with advice and prayer

Always add examples

Reconciliation

Saying sorry and having it accepted. All religions teach the importance of forgiveness

'Making up' and starting together again. Many faith communities have reconciliation services

When things go wrong

What can religious communities do when things start to go wrong in a marriage?

- The religious leader can offer help and advice to the couple.
- The community can offer marriage guidance counselling or therapy sessions.
- Older and more experienced couples could talk with and support the couple having problems.
- Family members could offer help and advice, especially in those religions where families have a specific role.
- Prayers can be offered for or with the couple.
- A group of 'young married couples' could meet, to help discuss and share experiences and learning.
- A pre-marriage course could be offered for all intending to get married.
- A booklet or leaflet with religious teaching about marriage and family life could be prepared and given to couples when they marry.

Exam Tip

When answering a question that asks for a point of view you must give good evidence to back it up. This should include religious teaching or practice. You will be asked to 'show that you have thought about more than one point of view'. Many candidates lose marks because they state a view without any real evidence.

Q *'The best marriages are those where a couple fall in love with each other.' Do you agree? Give reasons or evidence for your answer, showing that you have thought about more than one point of view. You must refer to religious believers in your answer.* [8]

Look at the two answers below. Use the Levels of Response Grids on pages 123–24. Decide what marks to give to each one. Then, choose one of them, and rewrite it so that it gets full marks.

Answer A	Answer B
I do agree because if you fall in love then you really know that person and what makes them happy. Some religions believe it is important to arrange or assist the marriage for the couple and then it is expected they will learn to love each other. I know someone who has had a marriage like this and they are very happy.	I disagree because I think that you can't really know someone until you are married to them. You can fall in love one day and out of love the next day. Some religious traditions have arranged or assisted marriages where the families consider suitable partners. I think this is sensible as the family often knows what is best for you. Evidence in England shows that fewer of these marriages break down. However, some people would say that if a couple are in love then it is more than likely that they will stay together.

Point of no return

For many people, divorce is very much a last resort, when they have tried everything else, and still cannot make any reconciliation. Most religions have teachings about divorce and about remarriage after divorce.

Christianity ✝

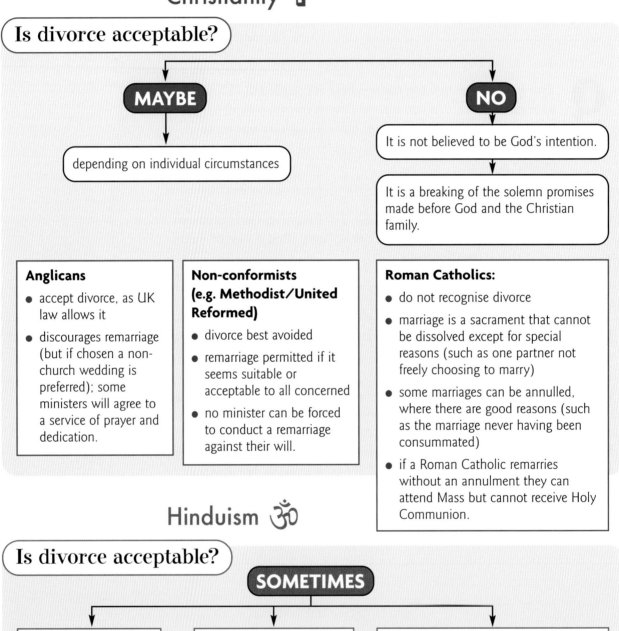

Is divorce acceptable?

MAYBE

depending on individual circumstances

NO

It is not believed to be God's intention.

It is a breaking of the solemn promises made before God and the Christian family.

Anglicans
- accept divorce, as UK law allows it
- discourages remarriage (but if chosen a non-church wedding is preferred); some ministers will agree to a service of prayer and dedication.

Non-conformists (e.g. Methodist/United Reformed)
- divorce best avoided
- remarriage permitted if it seems suitable or acceptable to all concerned
- no minister can be forced to conduct a remarriage against their will.

Roman Catholics:
- do not recognise divorce
- marriage is a sacrament that cannot be dissolved except for special reasons (such as one partner not freely choosing to marry)
- some marriages can be annulled, where there are good reasons (such as the marriage never having been consummated)
- if a Roman Catholic remarries without an annulment they can attend Mass but cannot receive Holy Communion.

Hinduism ॐ

Is divorce acceptable?

SOMETIMES

As a last resort, or the sacramental concept of marriage would be meaningless.

Hindus of lower castes have always allowed divorce and the remarriage of both partners.

But it is uncommon because arranged marriages are less likely to break down.

The extended family would support a couple in their attempts to be reconciled.

Islam ☪

Is divorce acceptable?

SOMETIMES

As a last resort. The Prophet Muhammad said: 'Of all the things which have been permitted divorce is the most hated by Allah.'

It is expected that the family will try to help the couple to be reconciled.

If the couple do decide to divorce then: The husband must state in front of witnesses on three separate occasions that the marriage is over.

A period of three months begins (*Iddah*). The couple will stay in the same house but not sleep together. (*This ensures that there is no confusion about who is the father of any children born after the divorce.*)

If the couple finally decide to divorce, then the wife is given the final part of her dowry. Both parties should act toward the other with kindness and charity.

Judaism ♆

Is divorce acceptable?

❛When a man takes a wife and marries her, if then she finds no favour in his eyes because he has found some indecency in her, and he writes her a bill of divorce, and puts it in her hand ...❜

(Deuteronomy 24:1–4)

YES → **BUT ...**

It is always a last resort. The community will give support and try to keep the couple together.

A religious and a civil divorce must be obtained by all couples outside of Israel.

The couple will apply to the **Bet Din**, the religious court of rabbis, where the judges will question the witnesses and give their verdict.

In the Orthodox tradition the husband is expected to give a document of divorce (*get*) to the wife. This dissolves the marriage.

The women is allowed to remarry after 90 days.

The divorce takes effect as soon as the woman receives the document.

Sometimes problems are caused where a husband has refused to give the woman a divorce, or where he cannot be traced; women in this situation are called *agunot* (chained).

See the picture about the 'Free the Agunot' campaign and prayer for Agunot on the next page.

Jewish Agunot women demonstrating

Prayer for Agunot
(*written by the International Coalition of Agunah Rights*)

Creator of Heaven and Earth,
May it be your will to free the captive wives of Israel,
When love and sanctity have fled the home,
But their husbands bind them in the tatters of ketubot*.

Remove the bitter burden from these agunot
    and soften the hearts of their misguided captors.
Liberate your faithful daughters from their anguish.
Enable them to establish new homes and raise up
    children in peace.

Grant wisdom to the judges of Israel.
Teach them to recognise oppression and rule
    against it.
Infuse our rabbis with courage to use their power
    for good alone.
Blessed are you, Creator of heaven and earth,
    who frees the captives.

(*Baruch Mateir Asurim*)

*wedding contracts

Look it up
www.agunot-campaign.org.uk

Buddhism

Is divorce acceptable?

YES → **BUT...** Making vows or promises is very important in Buddhism and therefore people should try to stick to them.

MAYBE

However, Buddhists realise that times change and it might be the best cause of action.

It is important that the divorce is for the right intention and not to cause further suffering.

Sikhism

Is divorce acceptable?

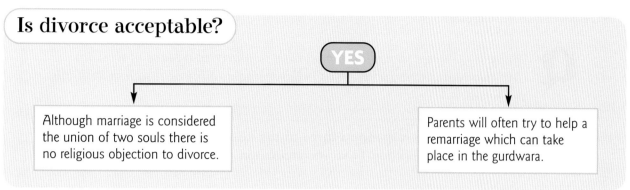

YES

Although marriage is considered the union of two souls there is no religious objection to divorce.

Parents will often try to help a remarriage which can take place in the gurdwara.

Where should marriages take place?

The church is a special place; it is holy.

People should not remarry in a place of worship because they have broken sacred vows.

It does not matter where the ceremony is, everyone just gets married for the party afterwards.

People marry in a place of worship because their faith community expects them to.

Should everyone be allowed to marry in a place of worship if they want to?

Same-sex marriages should be allowed in places of worship if they are religious believers.

Places of worship should not be used by non-believers for their marriage.

No marriages should be allowed in a place of worship if it breaks religious teachings.

It looks better on the photographs.

Task

● **Answer this question.**

> **Q** *'Same-sex couples should not be allowed to marry in a place of worship.'*
> *Give **two** reasons why a religious believer might agree **or** disagree with this*
> *statement.* [4]

In your answer you need to respond to three of the key concepts – chastity, commitment, love, responsibilities, God, reconciliation, community.

Tips …

● Remember the question is asking you to respond as a religious believer.
● Remember to give two different views; they do not need to be contrasting.
● Look back at pages 41, 50 and 58 to give further details to your answer.

TEST IT OUT

Here is a typical set of examination questions for this unit. Write out answers to them, trying to take account of the Exam Tips and information you have been given.

(a) *Explain what religious believers mean by love.* [2]

(b) *Explain how having a religious faith might influence a couple who want a divorce.* [4]

(c) *'You should only be allowed to marry in a church if you worship there each week.'*
*Give **two** reasons why a religious believer might agree or disagree with this statement.* [4]

(d) *Explain from two different religious traditions the teachings about contraception.* [6]

(e) *'Marriage is not important any more.'*
Do you agree? Give reasons or evidence for your answer, showing that you have thought of more than one point of view. You must include reference to religious beliefs in your answer. [8]

3 Looking for meaning

The Big Picture

What is the value of religion in a secular society?

How do people experience God?

How do people respond to God?

Why do some people believe or not believe in God?

Why do some people use religious symbols?

How do religious believers respond to God through worship and vocation?

What influences people's understanding of God?

How important is worship?

How important are funeral rites and belief in the afterlife?

Questions to ask

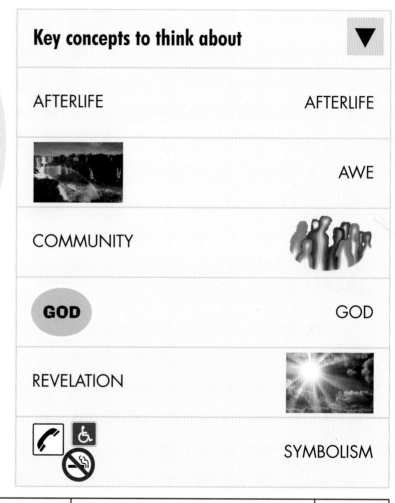

Key concepts to think about ▼

AFTERLIFE	AFTERLIFE
	AWE
COMMUNITY	
GOD	GOD
REVELATION	
	SYMBOLISM

Religious teachings to explore

- The nature of God
  – The nature of God or Ultimate Being
- The existence of God
  – Symbolism and imagery
  – Ideas about God
- Responses to God
  – Vocation
  – Acts of worship
- Religious teachings on death and the afterlife
- Religious funeral and mourning rites

What is God like?

Unfortunately there is nobody here to answer your question at the moment, but if you would care to leave a message after the pip . . .

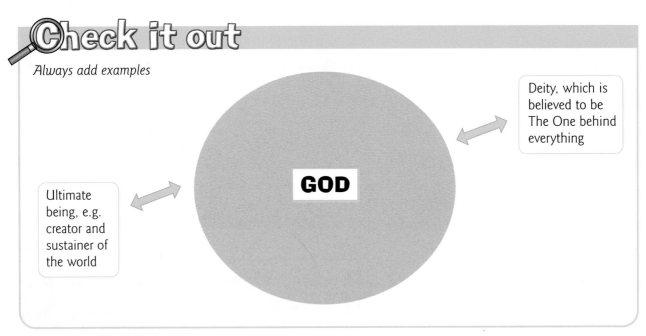

Check it out

Always add examples

Ultimate being, e.g. creator and sustainer of the world

GOD

Deity, which is believed to be The One behind everything

The nature of God

Many people wonder at some time in their life whether or not there is a God or ultimate being, and also what they might be like. Views often include:

A GREAT ARCHITECT! The designer of the world.

A JUDGE. The one who decides what should happen to us after death.

A She, not a He!!

I cannot believe that there has never been a God, an omniscient being who knows everything.

Like a FATHER. The one who cares for us.

I believe God is omnipotent, who has power over all creation.

People's views on the nature of God are often influenced by a range of things:

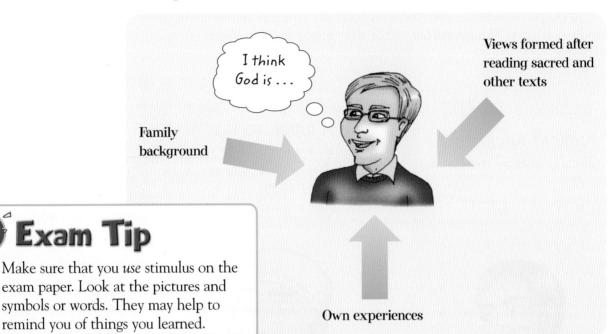

Family background

Views formed after reading sacred and other texts

Own experiences

Exam Tip

Make sure that you *use* stimulus on the exam paper. Look at the pictures and symbols or words. They may help to remind you of things you learned.

Q *Everyone's ideas of God are influenced by their family. Give **two** reasons why a religious believer might agree or disagree with this statement.* [4]

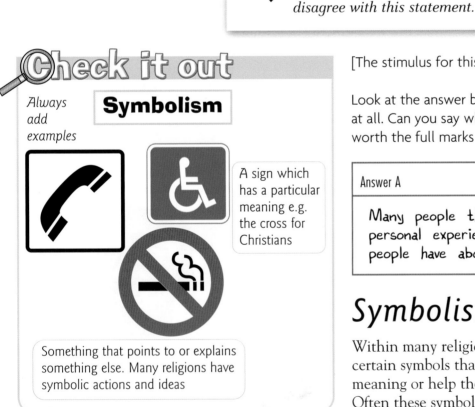

Check it out

Always add examples

Symbolism

A sign which has a particular meaning e.g. the cross for Christians

Something that points to or explains something else. Many religions have symbolic actions and ideas

[The stimulus for this question is the diagram above.]

Look at the answer below. It would not gain any marks at all. Can you say why? Change the answer so that it is worth the full marks for this question.

Answer A

Many people think that families and personal experiences influence the ideas people have about God.

Symbolism and imagery

Within many religions believers will wear or use certain symbols that they consider have a deeper meaning or help them express their belief in God. Often these symbols are considered sacred by the believers and can be used to aid worship.

Christianity ✠

The Cross

Christians believe that Jesus is the best way that people can know about God. So the cross, which is a reminder of the death and resurrection of Jesus, is a helpful reminder of beliefs in God and his character.

Christians believe that God is One, but is known or experienced through three distinct persons: Father, Son and Holy Spirit. They call this 'The Trinity'.

Christians do not pretend that this belief is easy to understand or explain, but many different examples are used to help understanding.

'Water' is one of the most common ideas used to explain Trinity. The chemical formula for water is H_2O, but as water it is in liquid form. H_2O is also a solid, which we call ice, and also a gas or vapour, which we call steam. Ice, steam and water are very different things – but each is still H_2O.

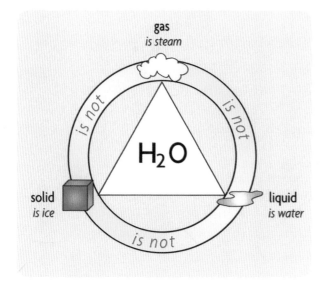

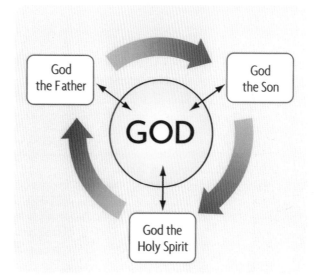

So with the Trinity, although there are three 'persons', the three are God-as-one. Each 'person' is an aspect of God's nature which humans are able to perceive and begin to understand.

In this way, Christians believe that God is Three-in-One. But the most complete revelation of God, say Christians, is through Jesus Christ. They believe him to be God's Son, born of the Virgin Mary, and yet also a human being – 'God in the flesh'. This was how he was able to 'reveal' to people something of God's true nature.

God loved the world so much that he gave his only Son so that whoever believes in him may not be lost, but have eternal life.

(John 3:16)

Christians believe that Jesus' death on the cross was the greatest act of love, as he gave himself up to die for all people. His resurrection on Easter Sunday was the overcoming of sin and death, so bringing new life and hope to the world.

As such, Christians call Jesus:

Meaning:
- he is equal with God, his father
- he is ruler of the world and of heaven
- the One who directs or guides a believer's life.

Lord

and also:

Redeemer

Meaning:
- the One who pays the ransom price to set others free
- the bringer of forgiveness
- the One who gives eternal life.

There are also many other titles for Jesus. You might like to try and find out what some of them are, and what they mean.

Hinduism ॐ

Murti

Hindus believe that Brahman is everywhere, the real self in all beings, and the Supreme Spirit.

Murtis are images of the deities on whom the devotion is focused. Most Hindus will have murtis of their own *Ishta-dev* (chosen deity) in their home shrine.

The *trimurti* is represented by Brahma – the creator; Vishnu – the preserver; and Shiva – the destroyer, so reflecting the pattern of birth, growth and death that the world is constantly going through.

Using murti in devotion

Islam

The Wise

The Creator

The Most Merciful

The Subhah

The One who gives peace

The Friend

Muslims believe in the One God, Allah,
from whom all things were created.
The belief in the unity of Allah is called
tawhid. In the revelation of the Qur'an,
Allah is given 99 attributes or names.
Many Muslims use a *subhah* which is a
string of 99 beads. Each bead represents
one of the qualities of Allah. Many
Muslims use the beads daily as an aid to
worship.

The Eternal

The Light

The One who gives life

The One who gives death

The Protector

Using a subhah

Judaism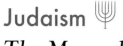

The Mezuzah

The belief in the oneness of God in Judaism is found in
the Shema which is recited by many Jews in the evening
and morning services. The first paragraph comes from
Deuteronomy 6:4–9, and states:

> Hear, O Israel: the Lord our God is one Lord,
> and you shall love the Lord your God with all
> your heart, and with all your soul, and with
> all your might. And these words I command
> you this day shall be upon your heart; and
> you shall teach them diligently to your
> children, and shall talk of them when you sit
> in your house, and when you walk by the way,
> and when you lie down, and when you rise.
> And you shall bind them as a sign upon your
> hand, and they shall be as frontlets between
> your eyes. And you shall write them on the
> doorposts of your house and on your gates.

Wearing tefillin

Many Jewish homes have a *mezuzah* case on their front
door. In the case are the first two verses of the Shema. It
is also rolled into *tefillin* boxes which are strapped onto
the forehead and arms and head and neck for morning
prayers on weekdays.

Sikhism

Sikhs believe in the one timeless and eternal God. God is seen as everywhere and in everything – what they call *sargun* – yet he is also different and far beyond the created world – and this they call *nirgun*.

Yet despite this God is believed to be close to those who worship him; he is personal and accessible to everyone and anyone.

Ik Onkar

There are many 'names' for God in Sikhism, such as *Sat Nam* (eternal reality), *Raheguru* (wonderful Lord) and *Akal Purakh* (eternal one), but the symbol *Ik Onkar* – the opening letters of the Mool Mantra from the Sikh scriptures – indicates the central belief in the oneness of God.

Buddhism

Buddhism has no concept of a god. Buddhism is about the search for true happiness and peace for everyone, and is based on concepts and practical advice on how to live life in a way that leads to the ultimate – enlightenment. This is when a person is able to get rid of all greed, hatred, delusion, selfishness, ignorance and desire, and so live morally, having trained the mind and discovered the truth, by following the Noble Eightfold Path, which is represented by the eight-spoke wheel.

The Buddha, the founder of Buddhism, was the one who became enlightened, and taught others the way. He is not worshipped as a God, but as an enlightened human being who, through his teachings and example, inspires people to change their lives and break away from greed, hatred and ignorance – the 'three poisons' which affect so many people's lives.

There are also other Buddhas in Buddhism, and in some forms of the religion there is a belief that everyone has a Buddha-nature within themselves. Within Mahayana Buddhism, there are also those called *Bodhisattvas* – people who wish to become enlightened, and are close to it, but delay their enlightenment in order to help others to become enlightened.

One, all powerful (omnipotent), all knowing (omniscient) Creator of the world, creatures and humans. Triune – Father, Son, Spirit. Best seen in Jesus. Wants a relationship with humans. Will judge the world.

A living creator who sustains the earth and all in it; He is one, and is the only True God; He is eternal, and Spirit – not being in any form; All knowing; All powerful; the Lawgiver; Has chosen a covenant people (Jews), will send a Messiah; will judge the world, and resurrect the dead.

The One Supreme Spirit (Brahman); eternal and everywhere; impersonal one world spirit; is manifested (in essence) in Trimurti (Brahma, Shiva, Vishnu); also in many different forms; is male and female; saves the world through avatars of Vishnu.

One (tawhid); transcendent and all knowing; Creator of the world, including humans; Merciful and gracious; Requires submission to him in obedience; Sent his last and greatest Prophet Muhammad to lead and guide his people; will judge the world.

CHRISTIAN

JEWISH

MUSLIM

HINDU

God Is . . .

ATHEISM

SIKHISM

HUMANISM

BUDDHISM

There is no god in reality, other than in one's own imagination; 'God' is an idea from the past that is no longer needed to explain the unknown or mysterious.

God is one, and is eternal and timeless. He is everywhere and in everything; yet he is also close to those who worship him, and accessible to all. He is the creator of all things, but is above and beyond all of creation. God's will – hukam – is supreme and should be followed by people in their lives. Sikhs also believe that there is a 'divine spark' in each individual, and that each human soul is part of God.

There is no belief in God as a supreme or real being; this is seen as the remains of the past, and not having a place in the modern world. The future of humankind, and the happiness in and meaning of life, is to be found within the human spirit and being.

There is no belief in a personal god or Supreme Being. The Buddha is the one who gained Enlightenment, and shows the way for others to become enlightened. Buddha taught about the Three Universal Truths, the Four Noble Truths and The Eightfold Path – these were the way to work towards enlightenment, and conquer the poisons of greed, hatred and ignorance.

Task

- Draw a wall of ten bricks on a piece of paper. From the religions you have studied, write a statement about what God is like in each brick.

Why do some people believe in God and some do not?

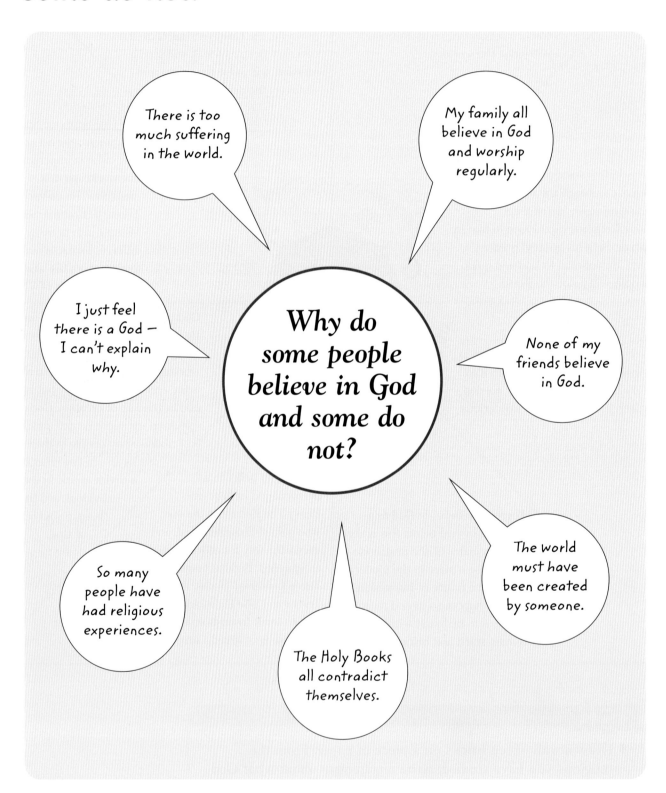

How do people experience God?

Miracle

A miracle is usually regarded as something that is a wonder, a supernatural happening; something that wouldn't happen in the normal course of events.

For many people, in different religions, something that happens because of prayer or faith that is 'miraculous' is an experience of God, and a sense of his reality and presence.

> This story is set in Zimbabwe before it became independent, during times of intense guerrilla warfare. People on farms owned by 'whites' were not safe, and great security was necessary.

On arriving at her parents' farm in a dangerous area of Salisbury, Elspeth discovered to her dismay that her parents had gone away for the night. She felt afraid but busied herself with chores until it grew dark. Just as darkness fell she found to her horror that she had left her washing outside on the line. It was dangerous to leave it out all night as it would let any wandering guerrillas think the farm was deserted, but it was even more dangerous to go out into the darkness. What should she do? She prayed for help and direction and God gave her a very clear thought: 'Go out and get the washing in as quickly as possible and keep praying all the time.'

She did this and got back inside without incident. The night passed peacefully, but next morning a security patrol arrived and asked anxiously if she was safe. Was she disturbed during the night? When she said she had not been, they appeared amazed. 'Then who was with you last night?' they asked. She replied that she had been quite alone. The officer then told her that they had captured some guerrillas who said they had been about to attack her home after dark the previous night and were watching from nearby bushland. Then they had seen her come out to take the washing and with her was an armed man, and the whole scene was brilliantly lit. She had been conversing with him all the while.

(from 'Guardian Angel' in *A Hand on My Shoulder* by N. Cook and V. Frampton)

Act of benevolence

Sometimes a miracle is experienced almost as if it were an act of generosity by God, like the grandfather who went on pilgrimage to Makkah, and escaped from a raging fire that tore through the tents in Mina.

I'm so happy to be alive. I feel that I've been granted a new life by Allah.

Worship

Many religious people feel they have a direct relationship and communication with God through their worship.

Worship can take place in a special place with other people of the same faith, or it can be in private as an individual. Worship can be through a set ritual that is repeated, or it can be through personal meditation, prayer, thought or other activities the individual person finds helpful or meaningful.

Prayer

For many people, prayer is something very real. It is a way of thinking about God, and feeling that life is different as a result of praying. Take the example of actor Paul J. Medford, who says: '*When I get in, I check my emails and often phone my mum in Barbados, because the time difference is right for her then. I pray in bed. I'm not deeply religious, but I believe that God makes all things possible.*'

An inner feeling

Sometimes people just feel that God is there, helping and supporting them, even when things are not appearing too good. The singer Gloria Gaynor explains: '*I'd quit singing because I'd become a born-again Christian and I wanted to know for certain what God wanted me to do with my life … I had no income, but during that time I wasn't concerned where the next meal was coming from, but I believed God would supply my needs, and he did.*'

Reading sacred texts

Many religious people find sacred texts have a special meaning for them at a particular time and moment in their life. As they read, they feel moved and inspired, and sometimes that the words were much more than just words on a page; but as if God were 'speaking' to them directly. Yusuf Islam said, after reading a copy of the Qur'an, '*A feeling of belonging ran through me. I was a stream that had found its ocean.*'

Natural beauty and wonder

There are many beautiful things in the world of nature – and sometimes a person feels a sense of awareness that there is a God involved in it all, somewhere.

How do people respond to God through worship?

Prayer

Prayer is a regular feature of many people's lives. Sometimes people pray together or on their own. In many religions there are particular times or patterns of praying that believers follow.

Preaching and teaching

Sharing the faith with others, and helping each other to grow in faith is an aspect of all religions too.

For many traditions worship is a daily experience – such as *puja* for Hindus; for others, it is a regular experience, involving gathering with others from the faith tradition to join together – singing, reading, praying, listening, dancing, reciting.

Pilgrimage

Many traditions have places of special significance, and believers make special journeys to them – sometimes alone, sometimes with groups.

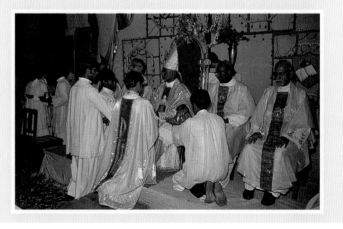

Changing lifestyle

All religions have 'rules' or expectations about the way to live one's life.

Service and commitment

Serving others may be a requirement of lifestyle. Many religious traditions encourage their members to see all that they do as a service, or a response to God and those he has placed in their care.

For many, one of the greatest responses to God is the commitments made by believers – they are prepared to give everything: time, money, experience, even life itself – to God.

Retreat or study

Sometimes, people feel the need to get away from the distractions of life that have a negative impact on religious faith and practice. So many traditions try to help believers by offering places and times of retreat so as to concentrate fully on worship, prayer, studying the sacred texts, or sharing faith with others.

Acts of kindness

Almost all religions commend acts of kindness to others, whether or not they are members of the faith community. Some religions expect people to pay a *tithe* (a tenth of one's income), or other annual welfare due.

Vocation

For some people, responding to God is a matter of what they do, in terms of a job or career, in their life. Some religious traditions have monastic callings – when people dedicate themselves entirely to God, and are involved in a life of service and ministry.

But for the majority of religious believers, vocation is in the way they do things in their everyday life – the sense of 'calling' they have to live their lives in a certain way – and this is their response to God or the 'faith' that they have.

> I owe everything to Christ; so I try to live my life for him, and in the way he asks. This is my calling as a Christian.

> As a Buddhist, I follow the teachings of the Buddha and live my life according to them. It is the middle way and leads to fulfilment.

> It is my responsibility to keep the mitzvot. This is my desire and it is my response to God. All Jews are called to keep the commandments.

> God is the centre of my life. After all, he gave me all things to enjoy; and I serve others too – it is my duty.

> My devotion to Krishna is my calling and dharma. Through it I serve my Lord, and all those around me.

> Allah calls all believers to worship him alone, and to look after the world; this is our duty.

Check it out

Always add examples

Community

A group of people with something in common; faith communities share beliefs and practices

A fellowship of people who pray and worship together

What is the value of religion in secular society?

> **SECULAR SOCIETY** – this is a term that refers to the way of life in countries where the government and general life are not led by or linked to religious people or organisations. It is something separate from religious beliefs and practices.

On the one hand …

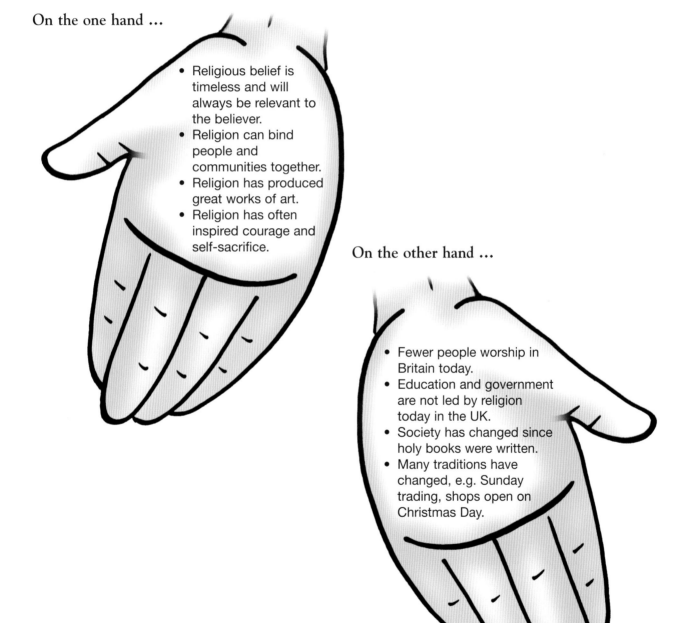

- Religious belief is timeless and will always be relevant to the believer?
- Religion can bind people and communities together.
- Religion has produced great works of art.
- Religion has often inspired courage and self-sacrifice.

On the other hand …

- Fewer people worship in Britain today.
- Education and government are not led by religion today in the UK.
- Society has changed since holy books were written.
- Many traditions have changed, e.g. Sunday trading, shops open on Christmas Day.

God isn't just for Christmas!

Task

- What do you think is meant by the cartoon?
- Explain **three** ways people could show they believe in God throughout the year.
  Now try to answer the question below. *(Use the SWAWOS framework! see page 18.)*

'The only true response to God is to offer worship and praise.' Do you agree? Give reasons or evidence for your answer, showing that you have thought of more than one point of view. You must include reference to religious beliefs in your answer. [8]

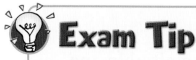 **Exam Tip**

It is very important to select the important points when writing an answer. Try to identify the key word/s in the question, and give specific and relevant information.

Q *Explain how faith might help a religious believer face difficulties in life.* [4]

Look at the columns of bullet points below. Select those that you think would be appropriate as an answer to the above question. Explain why the ones you haven't selected are inappropriate.

- God created the earth.
- All life belongs to God, who is in control.
- God gives people free will, so suffering and unhappiness result from a rejecting of God's ways.
- Life in endurable, and is not a trial; God gives strength to those who believe.
- A person's life is holy and sacred.
- Each individual is unique.
- With every temptation or difficulty, God gives a pathway of escape or success.
- After death is judgement, and those who do wrong will be punished.
- Prayer and worship often give inspiration and strength, and a sense of awe.
- God is loving and forgiving; and knows everything we have to go through.

Now select one of the other religions you are studying, and write a full answer to the same question from the point of view of that tradition.

Check it out

Always add examples

Awe

A sense of fear, and at the same time reverence

Completely overwhelmed by a sense of God's presence

Check it out

Always add examples

Revelation

Something shown or explained that was previously hidden. Religions have revealed truths

Something which (or someone who) enables others to learn more, or see something for themselves, about God, life, or eternity

Is that it?

Religious teachings on death, the afterlife and funeral rites

Death is a fact of life: everyone must die at some time. Religions all have different teachings about what happens at death and after it. For some these are revealed truths or revelations. They also have ceremonies or rituals to mark the passing away of the deceased.

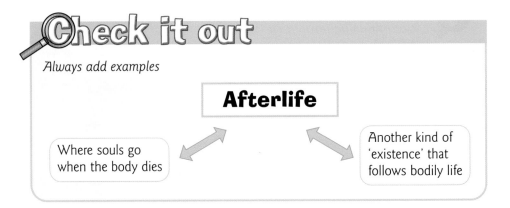

Check it out

Always add examples

Afterlife

Where souls go when the body dies

Another kind of 'existence' that follows bodily life

For many believers, the belief in life after death or the explanations about what happens or could happen after death, are important in making sense of life. For some it is a 'reward' for a life well lived, or the teachings of God or the leaders of the religion followed closely. For others, it is a redressing of imbalances and inequalities or unfairness in life. For some, it is the outcome of the life, worship and experiences of the present life.

But whatever it is, it makes a difference in the way the believers see life, and how they respond to the things that they experience and the issues they face. It is never just something that is to be thought about when facing death; it is something to prepare for, in readiness – for the one certain thing in life is that everyone dies.

For many people, funeral rites are important. They are a way of saying goodbye to the person and marking and valuing the contribution they made to their families and communities. The funeral helps to make sense of the experience of suffering and death in the world, and gives hope and meaning to those who have lost someone important to them, and whom they loved dearly. Different religious traditions have mourning rites to help people through this time of transition.

Christianity ✞

Christians believe that death is not the end, nor need it be seen as a great tragedy – for they believe that there is an eternal life after death for believers. They believe that to face death as a Christian is to have a certain and sure hope: *'Even if I walk through the dark valley of death, I will not be afraid, because you are with me.' (Psalm 23:4)*

Eternal life is received through faith. Although bodies grow old and die, Christians believe there is a life after with Christ in heaven: *'We Believe in the resurrection of the body and the life everlasting.'* (The Apostles' Creed)

Timing of an individual's death is in God's hands: *'In his hand is the life of every living thing and the breath of all mankind.' (Job 12:10)*

Entry to heaven is dependent on two things:

- how a person responds to Jesus and his teachings: *'For God loved the world so much that he gave his only son so that whoever believes in him may not be lost but have eternal life.' (John 3:16)*

- the way a person responds to those in need on earth: *'I tell you the truth. Anything you did for any of my people here, you also did it for me … Come and receive the kingdom prepared for you …' (Matthew 25:34, 40)*

Jesus also described heaven as a party, a banquet to be enjoyed (*Luke 14:15–24*).

Resurrection is the main theme of Christian funeral services – in fact the service usually starts with Jesus' words from *John 11*: *'I am the resurrection and the life …'* Ministers or priests may also wear white, a traditional symbol of life after death and resurrection. The resurrection of the dead is a central belief in Christianity – because of the resurrection of Jesus. Belief in life after death is also important for the Christian idea of justice.

New earth and heaven will be made after the judgement day. Sin, death and evil will finally be destroyed forever, and Christians believe that the resurrection of Jesus was a victory over death and sin that all believers can share for themselves. So Christians believe that, in a sense, heaven is already present in believers through Jesus' resurrection.

Afterlife is a spiritual existence. Those 'redeemed' through Jesus will be resurrected to this new life in the new earth and heaven. There they will worship God and enjoy his presence, and live without sorrow or pain: *'God will wipe away every tear from their eyes. There will be no more death, sadness, crying or pain. All the old ways are gone.' (Revelation 21:4)*

Life choices are therefore very important. Christians see hell – the opposite of heaven – as a state of being separated from God through one's own deliberate rejecting of God and his ways whilst on earth.

Living a life of love towards others is the way to receive the gift of eternal life from God. Christians believe that there will be a judgement; a time when Jesus will return to earth again, and separate people into two groups – those who have behaved in a loving way towards others, and those who have not. The former receive eternal life, and the latter, eternal punishment.

Interment (burial in the ground) is a choice some Christians prefer, although many will be cremated. For those buried, a cross or memorial stone may be placed at the site of burial (cemetery), and some Christians will visit the grave on the anniversary of death. For those cremated, the ashes may be scattered. In some burials, the coffin will be sprinkled with holy water, and the priest will say: 'In the waters of baptism *N* died with Christ and rose with him to new life. May *he/she* now share with him eternal glory.'

Funeral services may include a *Eucharist* (Communion or Mass); many Roman Catholic funerals have a Requiem Mass. At funerals, after the opening words from *John 11*, or a similar passage from the Bible, there will be some readings, and the singing of a hymn or two. The minister, or person leading the service, will say a few words about the dead person's life, and how they will be missed, and remind the family and friends of the importance of the resurrection and the new life that comes.

Ending the burial service will usually be the words of committal: 'Earth to earth, ashes to ashes, dust to dust: in sure and certain hope of the resurrection and eternal life through our Lord Jesus Christ, who died, was buried and rose again for us. To him be glory forever and ever.' A service of cremation may have slightly different words, but the meaning will be much the same. Usually there will be refreshments for family and friends afterwards, where guests will share in their sorrows, and also their memories and beliefs.

Hinduism ॐ

Hindus believe that for the majority of people this is not their first life, but their soul has been reincarnated from a previous body. Death is considered as a doorway to the next birth.

Retirement (*vanaprastha*) or renunciation (*sannyasa*) stages in life are expected to help Hindus prepare for death. During these stages Hindus may concentrate on spending more time with their family, doing charity work, going on pilgrimages or renouncing worldly possessions and ties.

Euthanasia and artificial extensions of life are disapproved of – there should be a natural end.

Immediate family will normally carry out any rituals needed once the death has happened. This includes preparing the body by putting water from the River Ganges on a tulsi leaf into the mouth. The *antyyesti* (death rituals) allow the family to say goodbye and express their emotions.

Next day the funeral should take place. The ceremony is usually led by the priest and the eldest son.

Cremation is always preferred as it helps to release the *atman* (soul). Hindus consider their life as a sacrifice and this is the final sacrifice. Only *sadhus* (holy men) and children may be buried.

Ashes should be scattered in running water. Many Hindus try to take the ashes to spread on the River Ganges.

Rituals help to bring peace to the departed soul. The first *shraddha* (paying respect to one's ancestors) includes a symbolic offering of water and rice cakes.

Near relatives collect for a reading of scriptures which stress that death is the door that must be passed through from birth to birth. '*Only the material body of the indestructible, immeasurable and eternal living entity is subject to destruction; therefore fight, O descendent of Bharata.*' (*Bhagavad Gita 2:18*)

Annual commemorations are held to remember the deceased.

Transmigration or reincarnation is the term often used for the atman leaving one body and entering another. It is believed to take place over and over again from one species to another depending upon a person's *karma*.

Eventually it is hoped that by living pure lives this cycle of repeated births will stop and the soul will be reunited with God by attaining *moksha* (salvation).

> As the embodied soul continually passes, in this body, from childhood to youth, and then to old age, the soul similarly passes into another body at death. The self-realised soul is not bewildered by such a change.
>
> (Bhagavad Gita 2:13)

83

Islam ☪

The Qur'an includes many teachings about *akhirah* or life after death. Muslims believe all that they do on earth will be judged and used in evidence on the Day of Judgement.

Allah knows the time of a person's birth and death long before they are born: *'No one dies unless Allah permits. The term of every life is fixed.'* (Surah 3:145)

Kindness is shown by sitting next to someone dying, to read from the Qur'an and help them recite the *Shahadah* – the declaration of faith. The dying person should lie facing Makkah. The *adhan* (call to prayer) should be the final words heard – just as they were the first. The body should be washed and prepared for the funeral.

Hajji (men who have been on hajj) will have the *ihram* (robe) they wore on pilgrimage draped over them.

Imam leads the prayers in the mosque and at the graveside. The funeral should take place within 24 hours after the death. Usually only men attend. The body is buried as Muslims believe the body should be placed in contact with the earth. The ceremony should be as simple as possible. Expensive memorials should not be set up.

Releasing of the soul happens straight after death. It is taken by the Angel of Death to a state of waiting until the Day of Judgement.

Angels will have recorded a person's deeds during their lifetime. This will include what they have believed, and how they have lived. This evidence will be used on the Day of Judgement. The righteous will go to Paradise and the unrighteous to Hell.

Hell and Paradise are described in the Qur'an. Paradise is described as a beautiful garden with rivers of milk and honey while Hell is described as a terrifying place of heat and torment. *'Those who believe and do righteous deeds are the best creatures. Their reward is with their Lord – Gardens of Eden, underneath which rivers flow, where they shall dwell for ever. Allah is well pleased with them and they are well pleased with Him. This is for those who fear their Lord.'* (Surah 98:5–8)

Judaism

In Judaism it is considered important to focus on what is happening during life rather than being concerned about what may happen in the afterlife. *'In his hand is the life of every living thing, and the breath of all mankind.'* *(Job 12:10)*

Reform and Orthodox Jews have different views and practices. Most Jews believe in resurrection of the soul, and Orthodox Jews believe in resurrection of the soul **and** the body.

Euthanasia and autopsies are disapproved of. Orthodox Jews believe the body should be returned to God in as natural a condition as possible.

Synagogues will play an important role. If there is no one else then members of the *Chevra Kaddisha* (literally, 'Holy Society') will sit with the dying person. These volunteers will help prepare the body. Sometimes a *tallit* (prayer shawl) with one of the fringes cut will be placed over the body.

Usually the funeral should take place within 24 hours.

Rabbi conducts the service at the cemetery, *Bet Hayyim*. Prayers and Psalms will be read.

Resurrection of the dead is believed in by many Jews. The translation of the Hebrew name for a Jewish cemetery is 'House of Life'.

Everyone present will throw a spadeful of earth into the grave to acknowledge that the body has returned to the earth and the soul waits for resurrection. Later they will wash their hands to symbolise their separation from the dead.

Care of the living is considered important. Close family of the deceased will stay at home for seven days and allow friends to take care of everyday chores. This period of time is called *shiva*, and allows people to withdraw from normal life, and grieve.

Tombstone consecration happens within the next year. At this ceremony the cover over the tombstone is removed, Psalms will be recited and a brief eulogy made. Usually stones are placed on the grave, not flowers.

Immortality of the soul is believed in by most Jews. Progressive Jews believe that only the soul will be resurrected, while Orthodox Jews expect the bodies to be raised as well. Jews believe that everyone will be judged and that those who led a good life will be close to God and those who have done wrongs will require purification in Hell.

Observance of the anniversary of the death (*yarzheit*) happens each year. Sons of the family will recite *kaddish*, and a candle symbolising the departed soul burns for 24 hours.

Names of the dead will often be placed upon plaques in synagogues so that the community may remember them.

Buddhism

For Buddhists it is important to have the right attitude towards death, for it is not something to be feared, but is a natural part of life, and an opportunity to progress towards enlightenment.

Recognising that all things are impermanent, and that decay is always present in the world, is an important part of understanding life and death. Buddhism teaches that people are always changing – physically, mentally, emotionally. This process of constant change leads to different lives and existences as people aim to achieve nirvana.

Escaping this endless cycle of birth, growth, illness, ageing, death and rebirth is the goal for all Buddhists. To do this, Buddha taught that people need to follow the Noble Eightfold Path. Everyone has the ability to follow the Path and to achieve nirvana.

Bad follows bad and good follows good is the law of cause and effect, or kamma. This affects not only the present life, but the life to come too. Everyone gets what they deserve, because of the way they have lived their lives; so the future is in people's own hands, and the rebirth that follows death is in accordance with the way a person's life has been lived.

Ignorance, greed and hatred all need to be extinguished in a person's life, if they are to achieve release and enlightenment. It may take many lives to achieve this, but each rebirth is a further progression towards the goal. For this reason, monks are often involved in ceremonies at the time of death, so as to remind people that life is impermanent, and we should not cling to it, and that it is everyone's hope to achieve nirvana.

Rebirth in Buddhism is not the person being reborn, but rather the kammic energy of the person who sets another life into being, with the kamma from the previous life going with you.

The goal of Buddhists is nirvana, which is not a place, but a state of mind – a happiness and contentment that is beyond the material and physical cravings of the body. Nirvana means 'extinguished' and refers to the 'blowing out' of the fires of greed, ignorance and hatred – the passions that entrap people into the cycle of physical existence.

Helping the deceased through transferring merit to them is done through special ceremonies or rituals that take place on the seventh day after death, and three months and one year after the death. Giving food and gifts of new robes to monks, and participating in water-washing rituals helps this process.

Sikhism ☬

A quote from the Guru Granth Sahib, the Sikh holy book, gives an understanding of the way Sikhs view death:

No cooking is done in the house on the day someone dies; it will be relatives and friends who take food to the grieving family, who are encouraged to mourn, but to stay calm too. Even at this sad time, Sikhs are reminded that their aim is to be focused on God, to be *gurmukh* (God-centred).

Every person is believed to have a part of God in them, and so they will also return to him. The soul never dies, it is immortal. So if the person has lived a good life, and has tried to follow the will of God and to do good works and acts of religious devotion, then there is the chance to gain *mukti*, or escape from the cycle of life and death. This may be after many rebirths, and Sikhs do not find this difficult, as they see the body as clothing for the soul; in death, the body is left, rather like a butterfly leaves the cocoon.

Washing of the body with a mixture of water and yoghurt is done before the body is dressed. For men who had been through the Amrit initiation ceremony, this will be in the *Panje Kakke* (the Five Ks). The dressed body is then placed in a coffin in the UK, but would be placed on a bier in places like the Punjab.

Death is seen to be within the will of God; it is a part of life for everyone. Death is the opportunity for rebirth, depending on the karma in a person's life – the good and bad deeds that they have done. During a service in the gurdwara, or sometimes at the family home, there will be a reading of the sacred scriptures – perhaps for a seven-day period (*septah*), or even a ten-day period (*dissehra*).

Ardas, the closing prayers, are said as the body is burnt, either by a fire that is lit on the funeral pyre by the nearest relative (in the Punjab), or at the crematorium in the UK.

When the body has been burned the ashes are collected, and will be sprinkled into running water, perhaps in a nearby stream or river. Sometimes, Sikh families in the UK arrange for this to be done in the Punjab.

No monuments or stone memorials are allowed in Sikhism; it is thought much better to remember the person for the good things they did in their lives, and in the memories that everyone has of them. Memorials may become objects of worship or importance that detract from a person's devotion for God.

'The dawn of a new day is the message of a sunset.
Earth is not the permanent home.
Life is like a shadow on the wall.'

(Guru Granth Sahib 793)

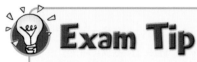

Exam Tip

When giving an answer about a religion's teachings or practices, be sure to give specific examples. Too many candidates do not explain key beliefs and teachings clearly.

Q *Explain the teaching about the afterlife from **two** religious traditions.* [6]

Look at the two answers below. Neither of them has given a full answer. Can you explain why? Choose one answer, and amend it so that it would gain full marks.

Answer A	Answer B
(i) Christianity Teaching: When death comes you can go to hell or heaven depending on whether or not you have been good. If you were in-between you will be sent to hell for a short time to be relieved of 'bad sin'. (ii) Islam Teaching: When Muslims die, they believe it is important to bury the body quickly, because there is a judgement after death.	(i) Hinduism Teaching: Hindus believe in being born again after death, depending on how you have lived your life. So you have to be good to get a good life; or you might be born again as a dog or cat. (ii) Christianity Teaching: Christians believe that there is a life after death - when the person either goes to heaven (where Jesus is), or hell - which is a place of punishment. Your destination is based on the life you lead.

TEST IT OUT

Here is a typical set of examination questions for this unit. Write out answers to them, trying to take account of the Exam Tips and information you have been given.

(a) *Explain what religious believers mean by 'awe'.* [2]

(b) *Explain how religious believers might experience God.* [4]

(c) *'Everyone has to respond to God at some time or other.'*
*Give **two** reasons why religious believers might agree or disagree.* [4]

(d) *Explain from **two** religious traditions teaching about funeral rites.* [6]

(e) *'People who believe life belongs to God should not mourn.' Do you agree? Give reasons or evidence for your answer, showing that you have thought about more than one point of view. You must include reference to religious beliefs in your answer.* [8]

4 Is it fair?

The Big Picture

What is fair and unfair?

Why do people treat others differently?

What do we need?

Why are people prejudiced?

What do we want?

How should we treat others?

How does the media influence attitudes?

Is equality possible?

What should be people's attitude towards wealth?

Questions to ask

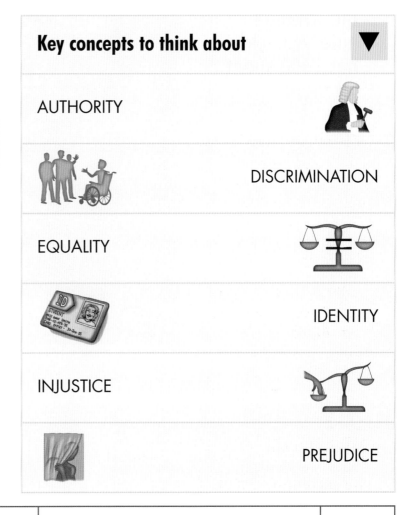

Key concepts to think about ▼	
AUTHORITY	
	DISCRIMINATION
EQUALITY	
	IDENTITY
INJUSTICE	
	PREJUDICE

Check it out

The definitions in these boxes in this chapter are basic outlines only; always add an appropriate example in your explanation, and remember the context is religious believers.

Religious teachings to explore

- Human dignity
- Equality
- Use of wealth
  - Charity
- Social responsibility
  - Religion and the media
- Religious commitments to promote justice
- Racial, social and gender divisions
- People and organisations who have worked for justice
- Religious responses to injustice

What is fair?

At Christmas the average nine-year-old has £600 spent on them

Task

- Make a list of things you think are unfair in *your* life.

'It's not fair!' How often do we hear this said?

But are these things really unfair? Of course it seems so at the time; but not when compared to the situations in other people's lives.

Most people would agree that **fairness** has a lot to do with having the same opportunities and rights as other people, and a sense of being valued and loved for being the people we are.

In the same way, **unfairness** is when those opportunities are taken away or prevented for some reason, and when there is dishonesty, and people are not valued.

Sometimes, there may be good or just reasons why not everyone can have exactly the same as others; but very often what prevents equality are the actions and decisions of people, politicians and governments.

Sometimes fairness and unfairness depends on a person's parents and place of birth.

All religions have understandings about why there is an imbalance in the world, and teachings that show what could and should be done to improve the situation.

Task

- **Now make a list of things you think are unfair in the world.**

Check it out

Always add examples

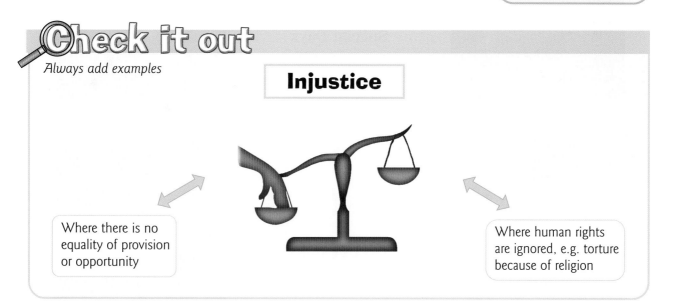

Injustice

Where there is no equality of provision or opportunity

Where human rights are ignored, e.g. torture because of religion

Check it out

Always add examples

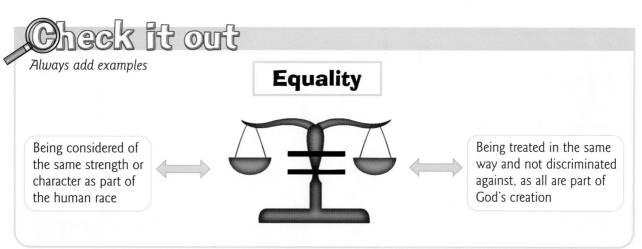

Equality

Being considered of the same strength or character as part of the human race

Being treated in the same way and not discriminated against, as all are part of God's creation

All religions try to achieve justice and equality in the world although some people would say this is impossible. Religions try to campaign against different types of injustices. Sometimes this has led to conflict with the authority of governments who allow these injustices to happen.

Task

- **Create a collage from the media that shows the difference between equality and injustice. Try to remember some of the examples – they could be useful in evaluative exam questions!**

Prayers

Organise
Special Days

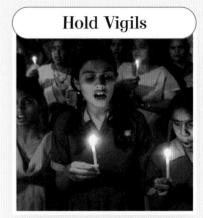

Hold Vigils

Fasting

We say: 'Justice Now!'

Collections of Money

Pressurise the Government

Organise Campaigns

Exam Tip

Use the stimulus provided in the examination paper to help you.
Never just copy words, phrases, nor simply describe the picture.
The stimulus should help you remember things you have studied or
discussed. It will give you ideas to write about and either explain or
state your own views and ideas.

Task

- Using the stimulus material on page 92 entitled *We say: 'Justice Now!'*, answer the questions, putting into practice the advice in the Exam Tip on the same page.

Q

- *Explain what religious believers mean by injustice.* [2]
- *Explain how having a religious faith might influence actions against injustice.* [4]
- *'All religious people do is pray. This can't stop injustice.' Do you agree? Give reasons or evidence for your answer, showing that you have thought about more than one point of view. You must include reference to religious beliefs in your answer.* [8]

Check it out

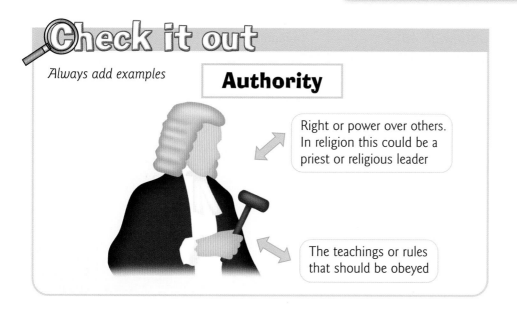

Always add examples

Authority

Right or power over others. In religion this could be a priest or religious leader

The teachings or rules that should be obeyed

Reference points!

All religions will encourage believers to speak out against injustice and seek justice. It is part of their responsibility to protect all **human dignity**. Believers will often decide how to act by interpreting the teachings of their holy books to put their beliefs into practice.

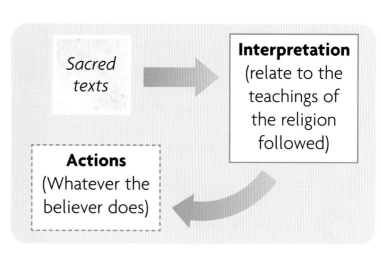

Sacred texts

Interpretation (relate to the teachings of the religion followed)

Actions (Whatever the believer does)

Christianity

TEXT

I was hungry and you gave me food, I was thirsty and you gave me drink, I was a stranger and you welcomed me, I was naked and you clothed me, I was sick and you visited me, I was in prison and you came to me ... and the King will say to you, as you did it to one of the least of these my brethren, you did it to me.

(Matthew 25:40)

INTERPRETATION

Christians believe that showing concern for others, especially if they are in need or treated unjustly, is a basic duty. Jesus taught that and demonstrated it in his own life, and expected his followers to do likewise. So one is not just doing the kind deed for the person who is suffering, but it is as if you are doing it for or to Jesus himself.

Helping others, in whatever way is needed, is a religious duty; failing to do it is failing God, and failing to live as true human beings.

The ways in which help and support are to be given are both simple and practical, and need not involve money. Kind and thoughtful actions are seen as being of as much value as gifts of money. The reason for helping is as important – if not more so – than the help actually given.

ACTIONS

Many Christians, and some Christian Churches or charities, try to give practical help to those in need, for example:

- Soup runs
- Night shelters
- Visiting the house-bound
- Counselling offenders
- Building and running hostels.

One of the most well-known Christian providers of this kind of action is The Salvation Army; but many other Christian Churches and individuals try to follow Jesus' teaching in the verse from Matthew 25.

 Look it up

www.salvationarmy.org.uk

Salvation Army volunteers talking to the homeless

TEXT
Whenever you did this (helped) for one of the least important of these ... You did it for me!

(Matthew 25:40)

INTERPRETATION

Christians believe that caring for others and sharing with others – in other words 'loving' them – is not only a duty but a command of Jesus himself. Jesus taught that all people have human dignity and should be treated with justice.

He also said that only loving the people who love you in return is not difficult; loving someone who is your enemy, or who dislikes you, or someone who is a complete stranger, is another matter. So Christians try to put this into practice in their day-to-day lives, and also support organisations that do it globally.

ACTIONS

Identify: *What is Christian Aid?*
It is a charity organisation working in partnership with local organisations in over 60 countries in the Developing World.

Mention: *Which religion does it belong to?*
Christianity. In fact, it is supported by more than 40 different Christian denominations in the UK.

Précis: *What are the main aims of this organisation? Christian Aid says:*

- To expose the scandal of poverty.
- To contribute to the eradication of poverty.
- To challenge systems and processes that marginalise the poor.
- To be inspired by the Gospel of good news to the poor, which promises a fulfilling life for all and the hope of a new earth.

Acknowledge: *How does Christian Aid work for justice?*

- To improve lives of people in poor countries.
- To support projects run by partners in the countries.
- To support the poorest groups of people, whatever their religion or culture.
- To campaign for fair trade and greater equality.
- To educate others into the causes of poverty and needs of the poor.

Consider: *How does the work demonstrate the teachings of the religion? Christian Aid says:*
It works on the basis of belief in: a God who loves the world and all who are in it; following the example of Jesus; speaking out against injustice as the prophets did. and the vision of the kingdom of God, which offers life and hope.

Tell: *A specific example of a long- or short-term project.*
In Senegal, Christian Aid works with local Cooperatives of Farmers – such as the FEGPAB* group at Diourbel. Here a number of active projects are funded by Christian Aid and organised by the FEGPAB management group:

- Farming and environment: including reforestation, animal fattening, producing animal feeds, building manure ditches.
- Training: including literacy classes (for women), management classes (budgets, etc.), and a theatre group to communicate ideas visually/dramatically to help the illiterate.
- Village water: well-digging (two per year) and irrigation systems.
- Commercialisation: to prepare for self sufficiency (through cooperative seed banks).
- Savings and credits: giving access to money through loans at low interest to allow trading and development.

(* FEGPAB is from the French for 'Baol Federation of Peasant Groups of Agricultural Workers')

See page 33 for IMPACT formula.

Look it up

www.christian-aid.org.uk

There are other similar charities:
www.cafod.org.uk   www.tearfund.org.uk

TEXT

And he made from one every nation of people to live on all the face of the earth, having determined allotted periods and the boundaries of their habitation.

(Acts 17:26)

There is neither Jew nor Greek, there is neither slave nor free, there is neither male nor female; for you are all one in Christ Jesus.

(Galatians 3:28)

INTERPRETATION

Christians believe that God is the creator of all people and nations, so everyone is equal. They also believe that humans are 'made in the image of God', and so have dignity and infinite value. As such, there should be no distinctions or advantages: all people should be treated equally as a 'child of God', and all should share with each other the good gifts God has provided in the world.

Jesus himself showed in his teaching and in his example that every individual is of value and importance.

Christians have generally spoken out against prejudices based on race, gender, wealth or condition.

ACTIONS

Impact: *What is Catholic Association for Racial Justice (CARJ)?*
It is a charity which works to encourage racial justice.

Mention: *Which religion does it belong to?*
It is a Christian charity, from the Roman Catholic denomination.

Précis: *What are the main aims of the organisation?*
- To raise awareness of the importance of racial justice.
- To understand human feelings of people from different cultures.
- To develop the theology of being 'One in Christ'.
- To tackle issues of structural injustice.

Acknowledge: *How does CARJ work for justice?*
- Education and publications – to raise awareness and provoke challenge and thought.
- Advocacy – to offer help to individuals suffering harassment.
- Holding regional conference and group sessions.
- Actively supporting Racial Justice Sunday (second Sunday of September) and the promotion of spiritual growth and development.
- Raising awareness and offering support to refugees and asylum seekers.

Consider: *How does the work demonstrate the teachings of the religion?*
The work demonstrates the belief that all people are 'One in Christ' (Gal 3:28) and the call to 'Love each other like brothers and sisters' (Romans 12:10). The organisation encourages Christians to: (1) Pray – and engage with the hard issues of racial justice; (2) Think through racial justice issues; (3) Take action that truly makes a difference; (4) Raise funds for local and national initiatives.

Tell: *A specific example of a long- or short-term project.*
CARJ has raised an awareness of the needs of refugees and asylum seekers entering into the UK.

Branches have responded in different ways. For example, in Cardiff Archdiocese, some schools held a Racial Justice Week with the chosen theme of 'Refugees'. Speakers came from a variety of organisations, and schools held liturgies, and produced booklets written by pupils. In Nottingham, members joined local council groups to befriend refugees, provide items of clothing, circulate press statements condemning the inflammatory language of politicians, and took part in radio interviews. A factsheet was distributed focusing on myths and misinformation about refugees.

CARJ also works with other organisations in promoting Racial Justice Sunday (e.g. Evangelical Christians for Racial Justice (ECRJ); Christians for Racial Justice (CRJ); and the Churches Commission for Racial Justice (CCRJ).

Look it up

www.carj.org.uk

Hinduism

TEXT
Perform your prescribed duty which is better than not working. Whoever does not work will not succeed even in keeping his body in good repair.

(Bhagavad Gita 3:18)

INTERPRETATION
Hinduism teaches that all people are spiritually equal, but that there are different duties in life (*dharma*) that people need to fulfil and accept as they are a result of actions in a previous life (*karma*). The dharma or duties will depend upon the *varnas* or divisions they are born into.

Some Hindus believe each person belongs to the same varna for the whole of their lives. Within each varna there are smaller groups called *jatis*. In addition to the four varnas there is a fifth group, which today are called *dalits* (oppressed). They used to be known as 'untouchables', and were considered to be unclean. They had to live in poor conditions and were not allowed to worship in the temples or use village wells.

ACTIONS
Gandhi spoke out against untouchability and renamed the untouchables 'Harijans' (Children of God). In 1948 a law was passed to abolish untouchability.

He said: *'I would far rather that Hinduism died than untouchability lived.'*

There are four main *varnas*:
    Brahmins (priests)
    Kshatnyas (warriors)
    Vaishyas (trade and skilled workers)
    Shudras (unskilled workers).
Each *varna* is subdivided into *jatis*.
The *harijans* or *dalits* are often referred to as 'outcastes'.

Many dalits live in poor conditions

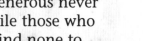

TEXT

The gods have not ordained hunger to be our death: even to the well-fed death comes in various shapes. The richest of those who are generous never waste away, while those who will not give find none to comfort them.

(Rig Veda 10:117)

INTERPRETATION

Like all other possessions Hindus believe wealth is temporary and that attachment to worldly goods (materialism) can hinder people attaining *moksha* (liberation from the cycle of birth and death). Hindus believe they are not the owners of wealth but trustees of what God has lent them. While they are on this earth it is important to help others. One of the four aims in life for Hindus is *artha* – to make wealth to support others.

ACTIONS

Identify: *What is Food for Life?*
It is a charity project working in over 60 countries in the world and distributes free vegetarian food. It is the largest vegetarian/vegan food relief in the world.

Mention: *Which religion does it belong to?*
The International Society of Krishna Consciousness (ISKCON) – a branch of Hinduism – started and supports the Food for Life charity.

Précis: *What is the main aim of the organisation?*
To provide vegetarian food and support those in need.

Acknowledge: *How does Food for Life work for justice?*
To provide free vegetarian meals, companionship and advice to those in need. There are many centres throughout the world. Over 400 free meals are provided each day to the homeless in London.

Consider: *How does the work demonstrate the teachings of the religion?*
The project was started by Swami Srila Prabhupada, who asked followers to not allow anyone within ten miles of the temple to go without food. It only prepares vegetarian food and exemplifies the importance placed on hospitality in the Hindu tradition.

Tell: *A specific example of a long- or short-term project.*
During the dreadful floods in Mozambique whole villages were covered in water and entire crops destroyed, with land unable to be used for the next three years. The Food for Life Distribution Programme began by cooking and distributing food to the refugee camps.

Food distribution at Sandipani Muni School in India. For many of these children this is the only meal of the day

Look it up

www.ffl.org

Islam

TEXT

What will convey to you what the steep path is? It is to free a slave, or to give food in the day of hunger to an orphan, next of kin, or to some poor wretch in misery.

(Surah 90:12–16)

ACTIONS

Zakah This is one of the pillars of Islam, and the compulsory payment of money or possessions to help the poor and needy. It is considered an act of worship (*ibadah*). Each year a Muslim will give about 2.5 per cent of savings to support the needs of others. Each mosque will have a collecting box and a committee to decide how the money should be spent. Through this system the whole ummah is made more equal.

INTERPRETATION

Muslims believe that Allah is the Creator of all humankind, and therefore they must take responsibility and care for others. The community of believers (*ummah*) are expected to care for each other. All wealth is a gift from Allah and so it is important that it is used wisely. A Muslim should not hoard money, or charge interest.

Muslims are encouraged to show care and concern for others in voluntary and compulsory action and giving. *Sadaqah* is voluntary charity given out of kindness. The Prophet Muhammad said that every act done to please Allah or make life more pleasant was sadaqah. Islamic Relief and Red Crescent use money collected by sadaqah in international disasters.

Muslims collecting Zakah

Islamic Relief worldwide

TEXT

Believers, stand up firmly for justice, as witnesses for Allah, even though it be against yourselves, or your parents or relations, whether the person is rich or poor. Allah is closer to him than you are. Do not be led by passion, lest you should swerve from the truth. If you twist or turn from justice, Allah is well aware of what you do.

(Surah 4:135)

INTERPRETATION

Muslims have always considered it important to speak out against injustices. The Prophet Muhammad spoke out against a range of injustices against animals, the poor and widows. He himself married Khadijah, a woman who had been twice widowed.

ACTIONS

Identify: *What is Islamic Relief?*
It is a charity which supports the poorest people in the world.

Mention: *Which religion does it belong to?* Islam

Précis: *What is the main aim of the organisation?*
To help the suffering of the world's poorest people through long- and short-term aid. It works with all people of all religions and races.

Acknowledge: *How does Islamic Relief work for justice?*
As well as responding to disasters and emergencies it promotes justice through:

- Promoting sustainable livelihoods to ensure people are paid a fair price for their work.
- Education for people who are normally too poor to go to school.
- Support for heath programmes particularly to make people aware of AIDS.
- Support for children who have been made orphans.

Consider: *How does the work demonstrate the teachings of the religion?*
It aims to give immediate relief and also to educate poor people to help create a more equal world. Their work demonstrates the concept of 'ummah' – community – and the teaching from the Qur'an: 'Whoever saved a life, it would be as if he saved the life of all mankind.' (Surah 5:32)

Tell: *A specific example of a long- or short-term project.*
When there were serious floods in Gloucester one summer, Islamic Relief workers gave out fresh water to people living in the flooded area, as shown in the photograph alongside.

 Look it up

www.islamic-relief.com

100

Judaism

TEXT

He has showed you, O man, what is good. And what does the Lord require of you, but to do justice, and to love kindness, and to walk humbly with your God?

(Micah 6:8)

INTERPRETATION

To treat people justly is as important in Judaism as it is to seek justice. There has been discrimination against Jews for a long time. This is called anti-semitism. The worst example of this happened under the leadership of Hitler in the 1930s and 1940s. During this time nearly seven million people were murdered. This is known as the *Shoah* (Holocaust). Since that time there have been many memorials to try to make sure such inhumanity will never happen again. Since 2001 there has been a Holocaust Remembrance Day in Britain on 27 January.

ACTIONS

The memorial centre of Yad Vashem in Jerusalem seeks to make sure that similar events could never happen again. It contains exhibitions of photographs, documents and artefacts. The Hall of Names records the millions of victims. There is a memorial to the children who died in the concentration camps. Here too is the Avenue of the Righteous Gentiles, where trees are planted to honour non-Jews who helped Jews during that time.

Look it up

www.yad-vashem.org

Two of the memorial sculptures at Yad Vashem

TEXT

When a stranger stays with you in your land, you shall not do to him wrong. The stranger who stays with you shall be to you as the native among you, and you shall love him as yourself; for you were strangers in the land of Egypt: I am the Lord your God.

(Leviticus 19:33–34)

INTERPRETATION

In the Talmud it states that 'Charity is equal in importance to the other commandments combined'. Charity isn't considered as merely giving money or helping someone, it is also considered as seeking for justice. Judaism doesn't just consider this a good thing to do but a *mitzvah* (required act or obligation).

The performance of every mitzvah begins with a blessing. Tradition says there is no such blessing before the giving of charity as that would delay helping human beings in need.

ACTIONS

Identify: *What is Tzedek?*

Tzedek is a charity which supports the developing world. It is based in the UK and began in 1990.

Mention: *Which religious tradition does it belong to?*

It is a Jewish charity. '*Tzedekah*' is the Hebrew word for justice.

Précis: *What is the main aim of the organisation?*

It has two main aims:

- To provide direct support to the developing world towards the relief and elimination of poverty regardless of race or religion.
- To education people, particularly in the Jewish community, as to the causes and effects of poverty, and the Jewish obligation to respond.

Acknowledge: *How does Tzedek work for justice?*

Tzedek has a number of programmes working in the poorest parts of the world. It supports the work of many projects in Africa and Asia. Wherever Tzedek programmes are set up, it is considered important to draw upon the knowledge of local people. Recent projects have included equipping pre-schools in a squatter settlement, funding environmental education workshops in Zimbabwe, and construction of schools in India. It has a threefold obligation to help Jews, to support the needy among non-Jews, and to care for the environment we all inhabit.

Consider: *How does the work demonstrate the teachings of the religion?*

The work of Tzedek is guided by and expresses Jewish values, understanding charity to be a form of justice. It follows the principles of Maimonides that 'the highest form of charity is to take a poor man into partnership'. Tzedek seeks to work with some of the world's poorest communities. Gideon Sylvester, rabbi at Radlett Synagogue said: 'Tzedek allows us to breathe the pure air of goodness, giving, morality and ethics.'

Tell: *A specific example of a long- or short-term project.*

An example of a long-term project is 'The Families of Children Project' which supports widowed and abandoned women in Bangladesh. As part of the project, Tzedek sponsors the cost of a craft teacher to help the women make a living selling hand-made crafts. It is estimated over 200 women will benefit. Apart from learning a skill they will learn basic numeracy, literacy and hygiene.

TZEDEK

JEWISH ACTION FOR A JUST WORLD

Women in a self-help group in Tamil Nadu, India, learn about health and family planning on a Tzedek funded project

Cows bought on a Tzedek funded project. The women sell the milk from the cows so that they can afford to send their children to school and eat three meals a day

Garden Party

Saturday 15 July

Raising funds for a School in Kamuli, Uganda

Entrance: £5 (adults), children free

Includes cream tea

Another fund-raising idea

Two Tzedek volunteers in Ghana 2008 with children from their school

Look it up

www.tzedek.org.uk

Buddhism ☸

TEXT	INTERPRETATION
Whoever in your kingdom is poor, to him let some help be given. (Cakkavatti Sihananda Sutta)	All money is considered an illusion. Everyone needs the necessities but people have too much wealth and become attached to worldly goods. It is important to help all to have the basic requirements of life.

ACTIONS

Identify: *What is the Karuna Trust?*
A Buddhist charity which tries to address the injustices that prejudice can cause.

Mention: *Which religion does it belong to?* Buddhism (Friends of the Western Buddhist Movement)

Précis: *What is the main aim of the organisation?*
To create a lasting change between the 'haves' and the 'have nots'. It provides immediate support and also programmes to try to develop the skills and confidence of people who are discriminated against so they can find their place in society.

Acknowledge: *How does Karuna work for justice?*
It particularly runs many projects among the Dalit communities in India. It also runs projects to build dignity and challenge discrimination against refugees, tribal people and street children. It has a four-fold model for supporting social justice:

- Meeting a community's immediate needs, e.g. building nurseries in slum areas.
- Helping discriminated communities to realise they have a role in society.
- Giving discriminated communities the power to campaign for their legal rights.
- Showing compassion in action so that other humankind understands the difficulties of some communities.

Consider: *How does the work demonstrate the teachings of the religion?*
'Karuna' means 'Compassionate Action based on wisdom'. Buddhism believes the things that divide people, such as race, religion and money, are all illusory and the more enlightened people are the more they will treat people equally.

Through compassion in action the Karuna trust believes change can be made. *Metta* or loving-kindness is stressed in the Eightfold Path as Right Action would mean treating people equally. Their work is always based on the principle of non-violent action.

Tell: *A specific example of a long- or short-term project.*
The Saathi Runaway Girls project supports homeless girls in Mumbai, India. Many females go there because they have no relatives or have run away from home because of abuse. In the headquarters there is a schoolroom, food, support for finding accommodation and medical treatment. After assessment the girls are given further education or vocational training.

Learning new skills to sell craft products

 ## Look it up
www.karuna.org or www.karunatrust.org

KARUNA
compassion in action

Sikhism

TEXT
A place in God's court can only be attained if we do service to others in the world.

(Guru Granth Sahib 26)

INTERPRETATION
Sewa means service and caring for those in need. It is an important part of Sikhism to serve all people no matter how rich or poor they are. Sikhs therefore try to put this into practice in their everyday lives, and demonstrate their faith through the service and caring of others that their religion encourages.

ACTIONS

Identify: *What is Sikhcess?*
A worldwide charity dedicated to creating justice by making a more equal world where everyone is able to reach their potential.

Mention: *Which religion does it belong to?* Sikhism

Précis: *What is the main aim of the organisation?*
To make positive changes by bridging cultural, religious and economic divides. The volunteers are of all ages and their aim is to make a difference.

Acknowledge: *How does Sikhcess work for justice?*
It takes an active approach by volunteering within the community. It began in Canada when it organised food packages for the homeless.

Consider: *How does the work demonstrate the teachings of the religion?*
It is based on three important concepts in Sikhism – equality, social justice and service (*sewa*). Sewa was begun by Guru Nanak Dev Ji to work for a common good for all. It should be performed without reward for the volunteer and is considered the highest blessing. Much of its work is connected with taking free *langar* (food) to those in need. It is based upon the principle of sharing, community and service.

Tell: *A specific example of a long- or short-term project.*
A Community Clean-up, which was dedicated to ensure areas across the United States and the United Kingdom would become cleaner and safer places to live. In Sandwell, volunteers cleaned up and removed graffiti from an area where many elderly people lived.

Look it up
www.sikhcess.com

Exam Tip

Sometimes examination questions in this unit ask for the name and a brief description of the work of an agency. **Always** mention specific things done by the agency – be brief and concise. **Read** the question carefully – there will always be a reason or statement showing what sort of agency or work is being asked for.

We believe in life before death

Many Christians individually give money to charities or help people near to where they live. They may also give their support by voluntary work, prayer, or gifts of money.

just one world

Look it up

www.tearfund.org
www.cafod.org.uk
www.christiansaware.co.uk
www.christian-aid.org.uk
www.traidcraft.co.uk
www.mayc.info
(This site, of the Methodist Association of Youth Clubs has a lot of material on wealth, poverty and debt relief.)

Check it out

Always add examples

Identity

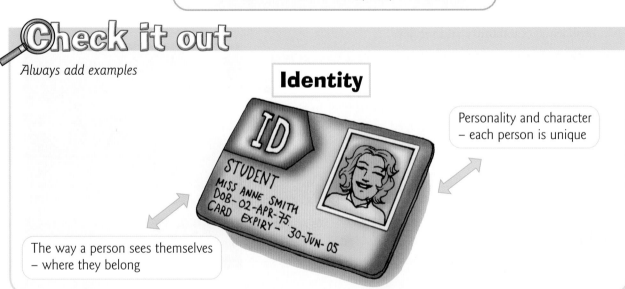

Personality and character – each person is unique

The way a person sees themselves – where they belong

Why are people prejudiced?

Check it out

Always add examples

Prejudice

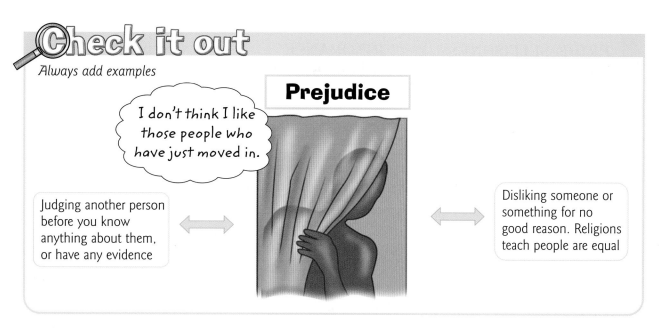

I don't think I like those people who have just moved in.

Judging another person before you know anything about them, or have any evidence

Disliking someone or something for no good reason. Religions teach people are equal

Check it out

Always add examples

Discrimination

Treating people differently because of race, gender, religion, class, etc

Failing to treat people as fellow human beings and part of God's creation

 **Exam Tip**

Always understand key concepts. Marks are often lost because there is confusion about prejudice and discrimination. Remember – prejudice is pre-judging; discrimination is the action.

Why do people treat others differently?

PRIDE/SELFISHNESS
Thinking only of self or self-interest; failing to consider the needs of others; jealous of others.

IGNORANCE
Not knowing or not wanting to know the facts.

EXPERIENCES
Having had an unpleasant experience previously with a particular group of people, or a person from that group.

FEAR
Being uncertain of the implications of others; not sure of the purposes of others; afraid of what might happen.

Reasons for Prejudice

THEOLOGY
Failing to see and believe that all humans are equal in value in their own right.

ANGER/RETALIATION
Reacting after some event or tragedy, thought to be the fault of a particular group of people.

PARENTAL/PEER PRESSURE
Accepting the views and attitudes of others without questioning or challenging; not thinking for oneself.

Locally, nationally and internationally there are many examples of prejudice and discrimination, despite all the religious teachings about equality and human dignity.

ISLAM

The teachings of Islam include:

- All people are equal, though not the same.
- All people are important in their own right, as created by Allah.
- Muhammad's example (respect for women).
- The *ummah* (brotherhood) crosses all national, cultural, political, racial and language boundaries.
- The act of prayer stresses the importance of equality. Individuals stand as equals before Allah.

HINDUISM

The teachings of Hinduism include:

- Each group or individual has their own part to play in life.
- The caste system describes such roles, and need not be discriminatory.
- All human life, whatever caste or 'station', depends on others.
- *Ahimsa* (harmlessness) is a vital aim in life, and discourages discrimination.
- *Karma* (actions) and *dharma* (duty) expect believers to do good and show tolerance.

CHRISTIANITY

The teachings of Christianity include:

- Prejudice is unacceptable and is against Christian beliefs and teachings.
- God created all human beings as equals, whatever race, ability, or gender.
- The Ten Commandments give guidance on living in harmony with others.
- Jesus' example (such as his treatment of lepers and outcasts) and his teachings (such as the Good Samaritan).

JUDAISM

The teachings of Judaism include:

- All humanity is made in the image of God.
- All have the same responsibility towards God.
- Being a 'chosen' nation is not being above others, but having additional responsibilities and duties.
- Israel accepts Jews from all nations and races.

BUDDHISM

The teachings of Buddhism include:

- All people are equal and have within them the nature of enlightenment.
- The things that separate people such as wealth, gender and race, are all illusory.
- We can learn from the example of the Buddha who rejected the caste system and taught that all people were equal.
- *Metta* (loving-kindness) towards all beings is stressed.

SIKHISM

The teachings of Sikhism include:

- The Sikh Gurus stressed that God is the source of all life and so all are equal.
- The *langar* shows how everyone is considered equal and welcome to eat together.
- Reunion with God is believed to be open to all.

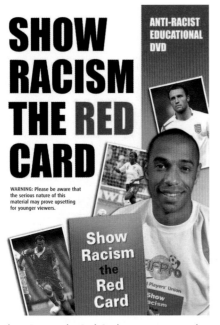

Three of the most common examples of people being treated differently are:

- racism
- gender
- social class.

RACISM – discriminating against a person just because of their race or skin colour.

GENDER – when discrimination against a person is simply because they are female (or male).

Look it up

www.theredcard.org

Show Racism the Red Card is an anti-racist charity which harnesses the high profile of professional sports people to educate young people about the dangers of racism

Although there have been historical interpretations that led to discrimination against women – some still persisting today – religious teachings also highlight the positive role of women in society. Often it is due to the culture of a country rather than religious teachings that women may be discriminated against.

HINDUISM

- It is mainly women who perform *puja* (ceremonial worship) in the home.
- Laws of Manu see women as supported by husbands, or sons, so not needing possessions of their own.
- The Indian Constitution recognised equal rights for men and women.

ISLAM

- Men and women are equal before Allah and have the same religious duties and will face the same judgement.
- Women are allowed particular rights and protection (to have no sexual harassment; be cared for in pain or difficult times; to be provided for; to wear the *hijab* (satr) for keeping modesty).

CHRISTIANITY

- Jesus did not discriminate against women (e.g. John 4: 1–30).
- Men and woman are seen to be equal before God (e.g. Gal 3: 28).
- Today in many Churches women are ordained and function as full priests or ministers.
- Women are unable to become priests in the Roman Catholic or Greek Orthodox traditions.

JUDAISM

- Women take an important role in religious ceremonies in the home.
- Women have held significant positions in Jewish history.
- Jewish identity is established through the female line.
- In some branches of Judaism women can become rabbis.

BUDDHISM

- Some Buddhist movements have nuns, although in the Theravada tradition full ordination has faded out.
- Usually women take part in all aspects of work, service and action in Buddhism.

SIKHISM

- The 5Ks can be worn by both sexes.
- Some Sikh women choose to also wear the turban to cover their uncut hair (Kesh).
- In the gurdwara women and men take part in the rituals and reading from the Guru Granth Sahib.
- Traditionally women's greatest role is seen as that of loving wife and mother.
- Women take on the name kaur, meaning princess.

Social responsibility and the media

Many people consider it is part of their responsibility to look after the weak or vulnerable people in society. There are many reasons why they consider it important to care for others.

Television and films show me how I should treat others.

I have learnt from my parents — they have shown me how to help other people.

My holy book tells me how I should act towards other people.

It's my own conscience that tells me how to behave. I have a feeling inside of me that tells me if I am doing right or wrong.

The media has an effect on many people. Many organisations are now making sure that the message given is a responsible one, particularly about bad language, violence or body image. The media is used to both promote and discredit religion.

Super-thin models banned from fashion week

What do we need and what do we want?

Life under the burden of debt

When people say they 'need' something – they often mean 'want'. It is very important to separate the two:

> **A NEED:**
> A necessity; something that is a requirement without which a person would be in poverty or extreme hardship.

> **A WANT:**
> A wish or longing for; something that is craved, but which being without would not actually bring hardship.

But Mum, I really need a new computer; I can't do half the things I need to on this old one.

Task

- What five things do you think are our basic needs to survive?

- What five things do you want – things you would like to have if you could?

Attitudes towards and use of wealth resources

Closely connected to the ideas of 'needs' and 'wants' are questions about wealth and resources.

Is this 'true' wealth?

I AM AN EXECUTIVE MANAGER, ACTUALLY!

All religions say that material wealth – money, possessions, status – cannot be of lasting value; they are all 'things' that can be lost, stolen, taken away, or can lose their value.

Religious teachings explain the need for careful use of wealth and resources, and that all that we have is given or loaned to us by God. Many religious believers consider people will be judged at death on their use of resources.

Where did I put it?

Oh no! It's been stolen!

I thought it was mine.

It is now worthless!

Christianity

Spiritual values are the most important:

Jesus said: 'Lay up for yourselves treasure in heaven.'

(Matthew 6: 19)

- Material wealth is not the most important thing in life.
- Do not worry or be anxious over money.
- Material wealth should be shared with others.
- True giving, or generosity, needs to involve cost or sacrifice.
- There is no success in relying on money or wealth for security or meaning in life.
- The way you make your money or wealth is just as important as what you do with it.

No unfair methods to get money

No greed or snobbishness

No lending for profit

No gambling

What about the lottery?

Many Christians are very concerned about the National Lottery, and the effect it has on people. They do not think that the 'get rich quick' idea leads to a healthier lifestyle. Many churches have spoken out against gambling, and so feel that the lottery is unacceptable. Some are also unhappy about receiving lottery money, and are concerned about the number of charities which have suffered through people playing the lottery instead.

A portrait

World Wide Message Tribe was a Christian pop group, based in Manchester. Andy Hawthorne, the co-founder, gave up an executive job with a large salary so that he could concentrate on the work of WWMT with young people. All seven members of the group deliberately turned their back on wanting to be rich and famous.

'We took a dramatic drop in salary,' says Andy, 'but in terms of fulfilment and satisfaction – there's no comparison. Life doesn't revolve around money; but what I'm doing lasts forever.'

As well as singing and visiting schools, the group also helped fund a special bus as part of the Eden Project, based in Wythenshawe in Manchester. This high-tech bus had comfortable seats, videos and electronic games, and enabled young people to have a good time, and to talk and think abut issues in life and religion. Members of the WWMT, and the Eden Project which it sponsors, believed that quality of life is more important than investment in money, possessions and security.

Hinduism ॐ

Material possessions are not of lasting value

- Wealth is not owned, it is loaned – by God.
- A person should fulfil their duty through their wealth.
- Personal wealth should be gained through lawful means – *artha*.
- If you are blessed with wealth, be generous and compassionate.

What's called worldly possessions is impermanent for by things unstable, the stable cannot be obtained.

(Katha Upanishad 2:6, 10)

No bribery

No dishonesty

No illegal means to make money

No greed

The gods have not ordained hunger to be our death: even to the well-fed death comes in various shapes. The riches of those who are generous never waste away, while those who will not give find none to comfort them.

(Rig Veda 10:117)

A portrait

Remember the Hindu charity Food for Life, referred to earlier?

Look back at the account of its aims and work, and write a description of how it interprets and puts into action Hindu teaching about wealth, and *dama* (charity).

Many Hindus individually give money to charities to help people near to where they live. They may also give their support by voluntary work, prayer, or gifts of money.

Look it up

www.ffl.org

117

Islam ☾★

Proper use of one's wealth is of lasting value:

- All wealth is a gift from Allah.
- It is not wrong to be wealthy; the more wealthy you are the more generous you should be.
- Wealth should not be used to harm others.
- Obliged to pay *zakah* (2.5 per cent of cash wealth).
- Voluntary payments (*sadaqah*) or good actions for charity are encouraged too.

A man who helps and spends his time and money looking after widows and the poor holds the same position in the eyes of God as one who fights in a war, or fasts every day and prays the whole night for a number of years.

(Hadith)

No usury (lending for profit)

No dishonest means to get money

No dishonest use of money

No gambling

Look it up

www.islamic-relief.com
www.muslimaid.org.uk

A portrait

Remember the work of Islamic Relief?

Look back at the account of its aims and work (page 100), and write a description of how it interprets and puts into action Muslim teaching about wealth and charity.

ISLAMIC RELIEF

Many Muslims individually give money to charities or help people near to where they live. They may also give their support by voluntary work, prayer, or gifts of money.

Judaism

Giving to those in need is a duty

Don't wear yourself out trying to get rich. Be wise enough to control yourself. Wealth can vanish in the wink of an eye.

(Proverbs 23:5)

- All possessions belong to God, so should be neither chased after nor rejected.
- A person should budget carefully so as to provide for their family.
- Many families use *pushkes* (collecting boxes); tithing is also encouraged.
- Wealth should be used for the benefit of the community.

No selfish use of wealth

No use of money on Shabbat

No greed

No dishonesty

A Jewish school in London raised funds to equip a pre-school in Zimbabwe

A portrait

Remember the work of Tzedek?

Look back at the account of its aims and work (page 102), and write a description of how it interprets and puts into action Jewish teaching about wealth, and charity.

Look it up

www.tzedek.org.uk
www.wjr.org.uk
www.jnf.co.uk

Many Jews individually give money to charities or help people near to where they live. They may also give their support by voluntary work, prayer, or gifts of money.

Buddhism

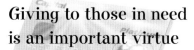

Giving to those in need is an important virtue

- The founder, Siddattha Gotama, left behind a life of riches.
- Buddhism teaches the middle way to aim to live between the extremes of having everything and having nothing.
- All material things are illusory and wise people should not be attached to them.
- It is important to gain money honestly.
- Giving money to others is one of the most important Buddhist virtues.

Whoever in your kingdom is poor, to him let some help be given.

(Cakkavatti Sihananda Sutta)

Gain money honestly

Use for good

Share with others

Follow the middle path

The Karuna Trust works with people of all ages

A portrait

Remember the work of Karuna?

Look back at the account of its aims and work (page 104) and write a description of how it puts Buddhist teaching about wealth and charity into action.

Look it up

www.karuna.org
www.karunatrust.org

'During one of my trips to the United States a very wealthy family invited me to lunch. I observed the opulence and comfort that prevailed in their home and I thought these people must be completely content ... I peeked into a half-open medicine cabinet: it was full of sleeping tablets and tranquillisers. I concluded they were not as happy as they seemed.'
(The Dalai Lama, *Beyond Dogma: the challenge of the modern world*)

Sikhism

Wealth has no permanent value

- Life's spiritual goals are most important, not wealth.
- Wealth has no permanent value.
- Money should not be spent on gambling or drinking.
- Service or *sewa* is important.
- Giving of time is seen as an important form of charity.

Wealth, youth, and flowers are short-lived as guests for four brief days.

(Guru Granth Sahib 23)

 No misuse of money

Earn honestly

 Sewa or service

 Share

Preparing food for local people in the langar

A portrait

Remember the work of Sikhcess?

Look back at the account of its aims and work (page 105), and write a description of how it interprets and puts into action Sikh teaching about wealth and charity.

 **Look it up**
www.sikhcess.com

Sikhs must earn their wealth honestly and share at least one-tenth of their earnings with those in need.

Q *Explain what **one** religious tradition teaches about wealth.* [6]

Look at the two answers below. Which of the two do you think is a good and clear answer? Why do you think the other one is not as good?

 Exam Tip

When answering a question that asks for an explanation of religious teachings, give clear specific points. **Never** write general 'cover-all' comments. Check carefully how many religious traditions you should write about, and write the **correct word** for the religion.

Answer A	Answer B
A Muslim is not allowed to receive interest on their money. Muslims are expected to help the poor by donating at least 2.5 per cent of their earnings to charity. Charity is one of the Five Pillars – zakah. Also your wealth must be gained in an honest work and effort; and gambling is totally unacceptable. The more wealthy a person is, the more generous they can be to those in need.	You should take as much money as you need and no more. Christians are also expected to be kind and do good, and to help others – whoever they are. A Christian should not be prejudiced against a person of a different race or nationality, and so should help them if they are in need. If they have money to spare then they should be willing to give what they can as long as they do not harm their own family through it.

Now write your own full answer to the question.

TEST IT OUT

Here is a typical set of examination questions for this unit. Write out answers to them, trying to take account of the Exam Tips and information you have been given.

(a) *Explain what religious believers mean by 'identity'.* [2]

(b) *Explain how having a religious faith might influence how you treat others.* [4]

(c) *'There is enough for everyone's need but not for people's greed.'*
*Give **two** reasons why a religious believer might agree or disagree with this statement.* [4]

(d) *Explain from **two** different religious traditions the teachings about equality.* [6]

(e) *'A religious believer has no choice but to campaign for racial justice.' Do you agree?*
Give reasons or evidence for your answer, showing that you have thought about more than one point of view. You must include reference to religious beliefs in your answer. [8]

Appendix

Levels of Response Grids for Marking

AO1

2 Mark Questions (question a)

Level	Level Descriptor	Mark total
0	No statement of relevant information or explanation.	0
1	A statement of information or explanation which is limited in scope or content.	1
2	An accurate and appropriate explanation of a central teaching, theme or concept.	2

4 Mark Questions (question b)

Level	Level Descriptor	Mark total
0	Makes no link between beliefs and practices.	0
1	A simple link between beliefs and practices.	1
2	An explicit link between beliefs and practices. Limited use of specialist language.	2
3	Analysis showing some awareness and insight into religious facts, ideas, practices and explanations. Uses and interprets a range of religious language and terms.	3
4	Coherent analysis showing awareness and insight into religious facts, ideas, practices and explanations. Uses religious language and terms extensively and interprets them accurately.	4

6 Mark Questions (question d)

Level	Level Descriptor	Mark total
0	A statement of information or explanation which has no relevant content.	0
1	A relevant statement of information or explanation which is limited in scope.	1
2	An accurate account of information or an appropriate explanation of a central teaching, theme or concept. Limited use of religious language.	2
3	An account or explanation indicating knowledge and understanding of key religious ideas, practices, explanations or concepts. Uses and interprets religious language in appropriate context.	3–4
4	A coherent account or explanation showing awareness and insight into religious facts, ideas, practices and explanations. Uses religious language and terms extensively and interprets them accurately.	5–6

Appendix

AO2

4 Mark Questions (question c)

Level	Level Descriptor	Mark total
0	Makes no relevant point of view.	**0**
1	A simple, appropriate justification of a point of view.	**1**
2	**Either:** An expanded justification of one point of view, with appropriate example and/or illustration, which includes religious teaching. **Or:** Two simple, appropriate justifications of a point of view.	**2**
3	An expanded justification of one point of view, with appropriate example and/or illustration, which includes religious teaching, with a second simple appropriate justification of a point of view (which may be an alternative to the first).	**3**
4	An expanded justification of two viewpoints, incorporating the religious teaching and moral aspects at issue and their implications for the individual and the rest of society.	**4**

8 Mark Questions (question e)

Level	Level Descriptor	Mark total
0	Makes no relevant point of view.	**0**
1	Communicates clearly and appropriately. **Either:** A simple justification of a point of view, possibly linked to evidence or example and making a simple connection between religion and people's lives. **Or:** Two simple appropriate justifications of points of view.	**1–2**
2	Communicates clearly and appropriately using limited specialist language. **Either:** An expanded justification of one point of view, with appropriate example which includes religious teaching and/or illustration **AND** either a second simple justification. **Or:** Two appropriate justifications of points of view linked to evidence or example, which includes religious teaching.	**3–4**
3	Communicates clearly and appropriately using and interpreting specialist language. An expanded justification of one point of view, with appropriate examples which includes religious teaching and/or illustration. There is also an adequate recognition of an alternative or different point of view.	**5–6**
4	Communicates clearly and appropriately using specialist language extensively and thorough discussion, including alternative or different views of the religious teachings and moral aspects at issue and their implications for the individual and the rest of society. Using relevant evidence and religious or moral reasoning to formulate judgement.	**7–8**

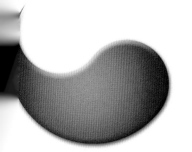

Index

Entries marked in bold refer to key concepts from the specification

Index